A DAMASCENE CONVERSION

A LIFE WORTH LIVING

St Paul's Conversion b

WILLIAM S. FLYNN, OFS

ISBN 978-1-0980-4705-4 (paperback)
ISBN 978-1-0980-4706-1 (digital)

Christian Faith Publishing, Inc.
832 Park Avenue
Meadville, PA 16335
www.christianfaithpublishing.com

Printed in the United States of America

To Our Lady of Medjugorje. For my healing and the many blessing, I have received through Jesus, her son. Without her inspiration and guidance, this book would never be possible.

I am deeply indebted to Father John Horn, SJ. For encouraging me to write my story without his continuous support and guidance, it would never be written. I am most thankful to Carol DeRoy, Claudia Shipman, Edward Kelley, and Father Joseph Torretto for support and enduring long conversations concerning this book.

The most beautiful and most profound
emotion we can experience is the sensation of
the mystical. It is our source of true science.
He to whom this emotion is a stranger, who
can no longer wonder and stand rapt in awe,
is as good as dead. To know that what is
impenetrable to us exists, manifesting itself
as the highest wisdom and the most radiant
beauty which our dull faculties can comprehend
only in their most primitive forms—this
feeling is at the center of true religiousness.
—Albert Einstein

Contents

Foreword

In this amazing book, Bill Flynn looks back in his life and invites us to marvel with him as he revisits many events and personalities to taste and see anew the mystery of the Lord's goodness and the power of his saving love. In doing so, Bill invites each of us to do the same. What transpires in our hearts when we ask for an increase of faith to review our own life story? Let us follow Bill's example and review our lives in that certain hope that we will taste and see the ways of Jesus's Spirit in loving us.

The landscape of Bill's life reveals an ongoing testimony to grace that is sure to move your hearts to smile and find new hope amid any trial. It is more than worth the read. A window to the graces that have been at work in Bill's life opens when we read about the reunion of Bill and his wife, Jackie, with their grandson, Billy!

Grandson Billy had been born to Bill's daughter, Ginger, in a surprise pregnancy outside of marriage. After supplying loving counsel and protecting Ginger from a man who was advocating a throwaway mentality that promoted abortion, Bill stepped up to the plate and provided the needed security for Ginger and her baby. Twenty-four years later, in a startling turn of events, the child (Billy) who had been raised by parents after adopting him through Catholic charities appeared on the scene. Ginger got to meet her son, and Bill and Jackie were introduced to the man who was their grandson. A banquet of love was described in their first meeting and throughout the years that followed. As readers, we receive awe. We are invited to feast on the human and spiritual nourishment that is engendered by being captivated by the beauty of real Christian familial love.

In his apostolic exhortation "The Joy of the Gospel," Pope Francis writes,

On the lips of the catechist the first proclamation must ring out over and over: "Jesus Christ
loves you; he gave his life to save you; and now
he is living at your side every day to enlighten,
strengthen and free you." The first proclamation
is called "first" not because it exists at the beginning and can then be forgotten or replaced by
other more important things. It is first in a qual-
itative sense because it is the principal proclamation, the one we must hear again and again in
different ways, the one which we must announce
one way or another throughout the process of
catechesis, at every level and moment. (164)

This is what Bill Flynn gives us through his creative writing.

This book reviews life in light of ongoing conversion. We see
the Gospel proclaimed in a variety of ways. The stories of conversion
call out to us in different ways to place our trust in Jesus Christ's
revelation of the Father's providential care in the midst of any trial.
Many short stories within the larger story of Bill Flynn's life serve us.
This narrative bestows upon us a catechesis for the human heart. We
are invited to absorb with laughter and tears, the truth, and beauty
of God's providential care. In a wide variety of ways, Bill describes
the hope that flows from knowing Jesus's risen presence at work for
us and in us so we will serve others in Christian joy!

I pray that you be blessed as you read by catching the conta-
gious faith that is contained within the testimonials that follow. Bill
Flynn generously shares his gratitude with us desiring that we "seek
first the kingdom of God...that we not be afraid any longer...for
your Father is pleased to give you the kingdom" (Lk. 12:31–32).

Rev. John Horn, SJ
St. Vincent de Paul Regional Seminary

Preface

What is a Damascene conversion? It originates from the conversion of St. Paul to Christianity on the road to Damascus. It brought to him a complete and everlasting change that deepened his belief in Jesus. In this book, I will attempt to share my experience of healing and conversion.

Few of us understand healings, but we know they happen and are fabulous gifts from God, rewards that come with significant responsibilities and many questions: Why did I receive this gift? What should I do with the gift? What does God want me to do? My story of healing from Our Lady of Medjugorje happened in 2004, and it changed my life and faith around completely.

It is not my intent here to prove healing or conversion has taken place but to explain in detail how they took place in my life. Therefore, actual medical dates and events are approximately close to their occurrences. I leave it to the readers to decide for themselves the truth and value of such happenings. To appreciate its value, you must be knowable of how my life was before the conversion. I must start at the beginning, the very beginning.

Allow me to share some things about my life.

Chapter 1

A Problem Child

I was born and raised in the historic city of Medford, Massachusetts, the "meadow by the ford" and the birthplace of Fannie Farmer, author of one of the world's most famous cookbooks; and James Plimpton, inventor of the four-wheeled roller skate.

Paul Revere had visited the city on his memorable midnight ride, waking up the city residents with "The British are coming!" His trip traveled along Main Street, continuing onto High Street in Medford Square. An annual reenactment would take place, honoring the historic event. The city, being about three miles north of Boston, was probably the third or fourth stop on his ride. He took a shot at each stop. The same was true for the reenactor. The square had a very sharp turn in the road before you arrived at McCarthy Funeral Homes, where the reenactor would tie him to the hitching post. And each year, we kids would bet that the rider would fall off the horse at that turn, which he did almost every year.

I was the youngest of three boys—John (Jack), 1941; Richard (Dick), 1942; and myself, William (Bill), 1943. We were the sons of two wonderful parents, John W. Flynn and Helen Francis Smith. It seemed I was troublesome to my parents from day one. I was born with hemolytic disease of the newborn, also called erythroblastosis fetalis, a condition that occurred when there was an incompatibility between the blood types of the mother and the baby. As a result, a donor was necessary to replace my lousy blood with fresh blood. The only possible donor was my mother's younger brother, Billie. Uncle Billie was a good man, devoted to his work and family, who loved life and lived it to the full; however, he had some strange ways about him. There was something to be said about genes, for it seemed I had inherited some of his behavioral manners, both good and bad. He had always said, "You are dumb. You know it, and you are proud of it." I guess he figured me out from the start. But he was a great uncle, and I miss him dearly.

I was born on the feast day of St. Nazarius (July 28), a martyr from the first century, so it would make sense that my parents would name me Naza or something close after this great saint. But they decided to call me Billie after Uncle Billie.

My middle name is Smith. I believe I was named after Gen. George Smith Patton because I was born around the time when he slapped a soldier in Sicily during World War II, but it was mostly because Patton's middle name was Smith, the same as mine. My name did not come from Gen. Patton but from—you guessed it—Uncle Billie.

Did you ever have a smarter brother? Well, I have two. As I mentioned before, I was the youngest of three boys, along with John and Richard. They both excelled in school; and I, well, let's put it this way. I was left back in the first grade. Who gets left back in the first grade? I guess I couldn't color and stay within the lines. My brother Dick claimed that I never stayed in school long enough to know my teacher's name. Both my brothers went on to graduate from universities—Jack from Fordham University and Dick from Lacrosse University—and I from the University of Parris Island.

I spent most of my life believing I was a nonachiever. Convinced I would never amount to anything and I was nothing like my brothers or anyone else for that matter, so why try?

As a youngster, my older brother Jack complained to my mother that when he would become president of the United States and live in the White House, he would be much embarrassed when I would drive up the driveway in my garbage truck.

A devastating event for my mother came on March 18, 1945, when my father was killed in action in Europe while fighting in

World War II. He received a Silver Star, the third-highest personal decoration for valor in combat. He was also awarded the Bronze Star for gallantry in battle in addition to the Purple Heart for military merit and for wounds received in action resulting in his death. My dad was a hero, a hero I will never know, for I was too young to have any memories of him. As I grew older and started going to movies, I discovered John Wayne, whom I adopted as my father. Had he lived, my dad would be just like him. No man could ever live up to the image I had created for my dad.

My dear mother had some trying times raising three boys on her own. But all in all, we were good kids; and I remember lots of families, aunts, uncles, and cousins being around.

In the early fifties, probably 1951, my mother met and married Lawrence "Bud" Howard, a pilot for Capital Airlines. He was a good man and a good stepfather, and they remained happily married until his death in 1989. Along with a new dad came a new half-brother, Lawrence "Buddy" Howard Jr. Buddy was two years younger than me, but he made a great playing companion in the absence of my two older brothers.

To complete our happy family, around 1952, my mother gave birth to the joy of my life, my little sister, Barbara Ann (Barbie). Barbie was and still is a pleasure for me. As a kid, I would push her around the neighborhood in a supermarket shopping cart, making believe it was a stagecoach, I was John Wayne, and she was the damsel in distress. Now Barbie was the one who held the family together, keeping me up to date with information and reminding me to call my brothers. What a wonderful sister for a brother to have.

Oh, I must not forget to mention my grandmother Bernice who also lived with us. Nana was my grandmother on my mother's side, a saintly woman who attended daily mass and was deeply religious and devoted to God. However, if needed, she would be a little rough around the collar. Nana had worked as a housekeeper in the rectory of our local parish. As young boys, if my brothers and I misbehaved during Mass, word would get to my mother via Nana, and we would be adequately disciplined. Nana was strict when necessary, even with the priest. The pastor had a nickname for Bernice: Burn Ass. Since I was the youngest of the boys and was around more than the others, I became her favorite, and I had profited the most from her wisdom. I believe it was because of her that I developed my strong faith. Nana was tenderhearted toward all her family, and I have loving memories of her.

Did I mention I was a poor student? Well, after being left back again in eighth grade, I believed I was just dumb and that anybody who was foolish in studies was differently dumb. So I started doing more stupid things. The first was quitting school and joining the marines.

A friend also by the name Billy had wanted to join the navy, so we marched down to the navy recruiting office, only to find it closed. The marine recruiter was open and signaled us over to him. "Why not join the marines? You both look like strong, healthy boys." He said we could join on the buddy system. "You will go through boot camp together and stay together for your first duty station." My friend Billy then claimed he "didn't think that we could make the marines." That only made me more determined. The next day, we were in New York City, taking the physical exam. I didn't pass. Back at the recruiting office, the sergeant said he had a friend in Newark, and off we went. I aced the exam.

The buddy system lasted only on the train to South Carolina. Once we set foot on Parris Island, Billie and I were separated. I didn't see him for over three weeks. Parris Island had a platoon for guys who could not make the grade and were on their way home. They would march them down the main streets of the base to the front gate and dismiss them, and who was at the end of that platoon? My friend Billy.

I loved boot camp. They told me what to do, how to do, and when to do it. I didn't have time to be dumb.

While serving in the marines, I didn't advance in rank, probably because of my lack of education or perhaps that I was a screwup. It seemed I had packed my negative attitude and had taken it with me. I survived my four years without ending up in the brig, and I did receive an honorable discharge. I guess I was what you might call a borderline-screwup kind of marine Lt. Gen. Lewis "Chesty" Puller would take some pride.

I was stationed at Camp Lejeune, named after Lt. Gen. John A. Lejeune, a war hero and the thirteenth commandant of the marine corps. Camp Lejeune is the home of the 2nd Marine Division that formed the ground combat element of the II Marine Expeditionary Force. I was a member of the First Battalion, which belonged to the 2nd Marine Regiment as part of the 2nd Marine Division.

Back in the sixties, the battalion was on a six-month rotation duty at Guantanamo Bay Naval Base in Cuba. In August 1962, my company was sent to Guantanamo or Gitmo, as it is most referred too. Guantanamo Bay, to me, was beautiful. The fence line provided a view of the ocean and a quarter of the island. I felt that the next six months would be like a vacation on a beautiful tropical island. Finally, a great duty station.

We didn't live in a barracks but camped out along the fence line. Our home was a hole in the ground, not a foxhole but a six-by-six condo we had dug out ourselves.

Life was good with three men to a condo. The only screw up I did was when one day, during a break from the towers, we had a campfire and was cooking dinner, and were having a good time. A sergeant told me to get some beans and cook them on the fire. When I returned with a large can of beans, I put the can in the fire without opening it. Everyone was having a great time, and no one noticed what I had done until the can explored and the beans flowed everywhere. The guys were upset with me because for weeks, they were walking around with beans baked into their helmets.

Once a week, we went down to the main base for a shower and bought what we needed at the PX. We decided to purchase a large transistor radio. With no electricity in our condo, we connected it to a large battery, and it worked; however, we had no reception because we had no antenna. The problem was solved by our sergeant. Thinking of ways to keep us busy, he became interested in our project. He suggested we borrow some ramrods and com wire to make our antenna. So we constructed our own, and it worked. Soon, we received a radio station broadcasting from New York City. I remember that we could get to the station only at night. We couldn't communicate with the station like calling to make a request. However, the station held a contest. "In twenty-five words or less, tell us why you like Campbell's soups." Well, one of my roommates in the condo would receive packages from home that almost always contained cans of Campbell's soups. They gave the address to enter the contest, and we responded, "We love Campbell's soups because it's the only thing we can get." We sent the letter as The Boys from Guantanamo. Well, wouldn't you know, we won the contest and started receiving cases of soup. After that, the station began dedicating songs to the boys from Guantanamo.

Along with the soup, we started receiving letters from young girls who would message to any marine who was willing to write back. There was no problem, and the mail started flowing. I was given a girl named Vivian from Rhode Island.

The fun came to a quick end on October 15, 1962. We were ordered to advance closer to the fence line and post guards at the towers. On October 23, President Kennedy ordered a naval quarantine in Cuba to prevent Soviet ships from transporting offensive weapons. The next five days were tense, not knowing if we would advance across the fence or not. We spent several days preparing to cross the fence line when the tense situation began to ease when on October 28, Khrushchev announced his government's intent to dismantle and remove all offensive Soviet weapons in Cuba. However, we remained in the towers for several more weeks.

On the Cuban side of the fence, they seemed not to be military but civilian men sitting around a campfire. It also appeared they didn't want to be there. I can't say they were friendly, but they were indeed not aggressive. The campfire men in front of our tower had an elderly donkey that kept braying all night, keeping us awake.

When the day came for us to leave the towers, a sergeant said that he wished someone would put that poor donkey out of his misery. I took that as an order, and with three shots (that day, I killed two trees and one donkey), I put that poor mule out of his pain.

Now naturally, I was bought up on charges that I might have extended the Cuban Crisis. But it came to nothing, and I got away with a reprimand.

Twenty years later, I was working for a liquor chain called Shell City Liquors. The chain consisted of fifty-two stores throughout Florida plus a hotel in Tampa. With many stores that size, it was necessary to have a maintenance team throughout the state. The team in my area of Fort Lauderdale were mostly men from Cuba. They were great guys, and I befriended one of them named Carlos. He became a great friend. One day, Carlos invited me to dinner at his home in Miami. He had a beautiful home and a beautiful family.

It was a wonderful evening. After the meal, Carlos and I sat and smoked Cuban cigars. During the conversation, he asked me if I had ever been to Cuba. I mentioned I was at Guantanamo during the crisis. He laughed and said he was also there on the fence line (he was one of the campfire boys). He said he had gotten along okay with us and that we were great guys, except one of us had shot his donkey. The evening ended with much laughter, and we remained good friends.

My next adventure came when we spent several weeks on an aircraft carrier. I was very excited, thinking I would see jets landing and taking off from the flight deck. We were surprised. It was the USS *Boxer*, an amphibious assault ship converted to a landing platform helicopter in 1959. There were no planes.

Life on the carrier was not a vacation. Sailors kept moving us from the portside to the starboard side. We spent most of the time on the lunch line. It appeared we were not the only troops enjoying this cruise. There were also troops from the 101st Airborne Division. Naturally, we all got along, sharing stories about our outfits and adventures, which were mostly lies.

Now we, marines, were very fussy about our appearance, especially our spit-shine shoes and boots. The airborne guys had a sergeant whose boots were like glass, for you could see your face in them. He would sit and harass us every day. "You, marines, can't shine boots like this." After a while, we had it, and several of us got together and came up with a plan. One of us would sneak into their sleeping department and steal his boots. The next day, one of us would parade across the area, wearing his shiny boots. What this would accomplish, I had no idea. It was a dumb thing to do, but I was part of the group, and I was still foolish. Not to damage the boots, we decided that the person whose foot size was the right fit would wear the shiny boots, and you guessed it. I wore the damned boots. The plan was, I would walk in front of the sergeant, showing them off. The guys would be behind me if something went wrong. Well, something did go wrong! Next thing I knew, I had four angry airborne guys, ready to throw me off the catwalk. My boys were not around to help me. I was on my own.

The sergeant decided to bring me up on charges for stealing his boots. They brought in front of my captain, who read me the riot act and ripped off my one strip, busting me back to private. Once we were alone, the captain wanted to know the names of my partners in this senseless act. I was afraid to tell their names, and that's what saved me. He seemed impressed that I would not rat on them, so he sent me away, saying I was dumb (surprised?) and that it was a silly thing to do.

My next duty station was San Diego, California. Can you believe this? I was now working in the brig as a corrections officer, not as a prisoner but as a guard. In the brig, things were very disciplined with rules and regulations. A spit-and-polish outfit with no way to screw up, we followed the rules which were drilled in us almost daily. For the next two years, things went very well—no trouble, no charges against me, and no screwups. I only did one dumb idea in the two years, and that was against a bull.

A friend of mine named Albert had a new car and was having motor trouble with it. He took it to a dealer to have it fixed, and they gave him a rental to use. Al had wanted to drive up the mountains of San Diego for a day of fun, so off we went. We planned for a day of adventure. We had lunch, a camera, and slingshots to hunt little rodents. About halfway up the mountain, we ended up on a dirt road. We pulled over to shoot and play around. All of a sudden, there appeared this huge bull. We managed to get back to the car and was about to drive off when I unwisely decide to shoot the beast in the ass with the slingshot. It was a direct hit, and it started charging toward the car. But Al quickly put the pedal to the metal, and we outran the bull. We got a clean getaway.

We continued on with our adventure for the rest of the afternoon, and when it started getting late, we decided to start back to the base in the same way we came from because it was the only way back. As we turned a sharp turn on the dirt road, looking at us straight in the eyes was the same angry bull, as if it knew we had to return this way. Before Al could put the car in reverse and hit the gas pedal, the bull rammed the front of the vehicle. I was sitting in the passenger seat with my feet on the dashboard. The angry bull hit so hard my feet were pushed out the windshield. The beast started attacking the car on its sides, rocking us back and forth. Finally and thankfully, Al was able to jam on the gas pedal and save us from this dangerous situation. We arrived back at the car dealership after closing and left the keys in a box and made our way back to the base.

I never knew how Al dealt with them over the damage. He never told me, and I never asked. And that was no bull.

The 32nd Street Naval Station is very near the Mexican border, so naturally, we crossed it to Tijuana. We enjoyed the people and the food and was always on our best behavior because the Tijuana police were seeking to control the military personnel who would visit their city. A lot of the boys would get drunk and unruly and end up in the Tijuana jail.

The only time we got in trouble was when my friends, Al and Jon, and I were partying in the city and decided to go back to the base. It was late and a long walk to the border, so we took a taxi. The driver looked like he had also partied most of the day and had a better time than us. He was singing some Mexican love song, and the cab started swaying to the left and right side of the road. All of a sudden, he hit a rock, and the door swung open. We couldn't close it. Al was hanging out the door with Jon holding onto his belt. I yelled at the driver to stop the taxi, but he just kept on singing.

The next thing we knew, a police car pulled the taxi over. The policeman and the driver were talking to each other in Spanish, and we could not understand what they were saying until he ushered us into the police car and took us to the Tijuana jail.

It seemed the police liked to arrest military personnel because they knew we had money to get back to the base, and they were right. There was a bus at the border that took us to the station for a fee. We would put money in our shoes and only spend what we had in our pockets.

They had a foreign policy at the jail that your fine was what you had with you, and if you didn't have enough, you would spend the night in a cell. In the morning, an officer from the base would come and arranged your release. We decided to keep our money and spend the night in the Tijuana jail.

Now to my next dumb thing: getting married. Not that getting married was a foolish thing, but it was how I got married. I just got out of the marines. I had no car, no decent paying job, and was living in a basement apartment with a friend that was still in the marines. We lived next to a nice senior woman by the name Carrie. She was accommodating and friendly and, at times, funny. My roommate, Joe, and I took a liking to her and would help her any way we could.

One day, Joe informed me that Carrie had a daughter who was now living with her. He said she was quite a looker and wondered if she was married or not. Joe was a very handsome young man who looked good in his marine uniform. He was what you called a ladies' man and would always have a beautiful woman hanging around him. So Joe was about to investigate Carrie's daughter.

Several weeks later, I asked him about her, and he said he was not interested because she was married and had a child.

There was a local restaurant where went to eat and drink (mostly drink). It served fantastic Italian food and was a walking distance to our apartment, so we spent many evenings sitting at the bar. One night, while drinking, I noticed a new witness whom I couldn't keep my eyes off. She was amazingly captivating, and something was happening to me that I didn't understand. Joe told me who she was and that I shouldn't get involved, but she was beautiful, and there was something special about her.

I took Joe's advice and didn't pursue my interest in her, but I couldn't stop thinking about her. I would see her almost every day, going in and out of her house with her little girl.

One day, at a local bar called Boots and Saddle, Joe and I were sitting at the bar, having a beer, when I noticed Carrie's daughter dancing and having a good time. I couldn't resist it. I automatically got up and asked her to dance, and she said yes. I was very nervous and didn't know what to do next, so I did nothing and said nothing. She broke the ice, telling me her name was Jackie, short for Jacqueline. I thought to myself, What a beautiful name for such a sexy girl. That dance stayed my mind for about a week. Yes, she was beautiful and was definitely interested. But I decided not to pursue her any further, for I had nothing to offer her or any woman. I had just gotten out of the service—no job, no car, not even a driver's license.

But much to my surprise, one day, she asked for dinner. I was astounded and didn't know what to say, so I said yes. For the next few days up to the dinner, I was a wreck. I didn't know what to do, and I wished I had said no. I had no money to bring flowers or candy or anything. The night of the dinner, I wanted to come up with some excuses not to go, but Joe kept laughing at me and told me to go, or he would go in my place.

I went and had a wonderful time. Carrie was lots of fun. And Jackie? Well, Jackie was the sweetest as she could be. I couldn't believe it was me sitting next to her and that she could be interested in someone like me.

Jackie's daughter was just six years old and was cute as she could be, but I got a little worried when she asked me if I was going to be her daddy.

I never had a relationship with anyone like this before, and I didn't know how to act. Fortunately, Jackie picked up this and guided me (she must have figured it out fast that I was dumb). The next thing I knew, we were engaged to get married. I had no intention of getting married; after all, how much did I know about her? I didn't even know what I should know about her. Getting married now was foolish. Here I was with no job, no car, and no future to speak of, getting married, taking on a wife, a child, and a mother-in-law. Isn't that dumb or what? And I never got to propose to her. She just said one day, "We're getting married in September." I said okay.

Fifty-four years later, we are still married and still very much in love. It must have been God's will. It certainly was mine.

It seems almost every family today has or knows of a rebellious or a drug-addicted child, and we are no exception. Denise was a troubled child from the start of our marriage. She was a lovely but angry child, and we as parents were not prepared to handle her. The child needed professional help, which I didn't understand at the time. The older she became, the angrier she got, and she behaved more aggressively. I was wrong in believing that love alone could help her. I misunderstood her anger, thinking that she directed her anger toward me. Eventually, she turned to alcohol and drugs and eventually disappeared from our lives completely. I will always struggle with a pang of guilt for the rest of my life for failing that child.

Not all was bad with Denise, as a teenager, she started dating a boy named Rick. He seemed to me to be a nice young man, and I liked him from the start. However, he reminded ed me of a character on the Jackie Gleason show called the poor soul. No matter what Rick tried to accomplish he failed. It was not because of his lack of trying and tried he did.

One day Jackie told me that Denise was having a baby and that Rick was the father. A beautiful healthy girl was born, they named her Kimberly. soon after that Denise disappeared from our lives, leaving Rick to raise the baby. He did the best he possibly could. He was a great father. I remember all the attention he would give her. We felt sorry for him in his situation and helped him as much as we could.

Eventually, it got to be too much for him working full time and trying to raise Kimberly (Kim) at the same time. He handed that responsibility to his sister Donna and her husband Jimmy. We would get to visit Kim almost every weekend, the visits became the highlight of our week.

Time passed quickly, and Kim grew into a beautiful young lady. Sadly, Donna and Jimmy decided to move to north Florida and that was the end of our weekend visits.

Surprisingly one day we got a call from Jimmy saying the Kim wanted to come and live with us, could we come and talk about this. Are you kidding, we couldn't get there fast enough,

The next several years were delightful. We totally enjoyed Kim living with us. But as children do, she grew up and the next thing we knew she was getting married. I wasn't happy with this marriage, but what could I say? Kim was happy.

My instinct was right and the marriage only lasted long enough to produce an adorable little girl named Madison.

It wasn't long before Kim met and fell in love with her future husband, a young man named Axel. He was a perfect gentleman and perfect for Kim and Madison.

One day while watching a baseball game, Axel asked me for permission to marry Kim. I answered, "why ask me, she has a father." He said that she considered me her father and that they wanted to get married in the Catholic church. I was overjoyed. Neither Kim, Madison, or Axel were practicing Catholics. Axel would have to attend RCIA classes (Rite of Christian Initiation of Adults) which he agreed to and did.

The following Easter Sunday was one of the happiest days in my life when Kim, Axel, and Madison came into the Catholic church. Next came the wedding. Axel proved to be the perfect husband, father, and son in law. Axel is now a pilot for Jet Blue airlines which provides an outstanding lifestyle for my girls.

Several years into the marriage Kim gave birth to another sweet baby girl named Kylee, now I had two joys of my life.

It is indeed a pleasure and a blessing to live long enough to enjoy your great-grandchildren, and we do enjoy them immensely, and I thank God daily for my extraordinary girls.

To ease some of that pain, God gave me another chance at parenthood when Jackie gave birth to a beautiful, healthy baby girl whom we named Virginia (Ginger). I couldn't screw this up.

Although I prayed and wondered where Denise was and how she was, I would welcome her home and beg for her forgiveness.

Ginger turned out to be a pleasurable child, a real delight in our lives. Finally, I did something right. As I mentioned before, our marriage continued for over fifty years, producing grandchildren and great-grandchildren.

Early in our marriage, Jackie had landed a great job with a phone company that provided excellent health insurance and income, which allowed us a decent lifestyle. I struggled to work different jobs—shoe sales, liquor sales, truck driver, etc.

In the early eighties, we lived in Pembroke Pines, Florida, and attend a storefront church, St. Maximilian Kobe Catholic Church. The priest was Fr. James Vitucci, a highly skilled speaker and a caring man who genuinely loved everyone he met. Father Jim would always remind us that God was in every person, good or bad. He would say, "If I can't see Jesus in you, I can't see Jesus in myself." He was a wonderful pastor who looked forward to death. He went home to the Lord on January 2, 2002, at age fifty-five.

Father Jim had a habit of calling me professor, so one day, I asked him why. He claimed I had the image of a professor. I began to laugh and said I had never stayed in class to know the teacher's name. After listening to my story, he said I was not dumb but only that I believed I was stupid. He advised me to take some tests at a local high school, and I did. The test revealed I had attention deficit disorder (ADD). I wasn't dumb at all. Thank you, Father Jim. It means a person with my brain chemistry has trouble and great difficulty in focusing. It was almost impossible to think abstractly and focus on what I was attempting to do. Father Jim made me understand that I was a much better person than I believed I was. He built up my confidence and made me think that with God's help, I could do anything.

This new confidence came into play quite quickly. When our granddaughter Kimmy decided she wanted a computer naturally, I purchased her one. Reading the instructions, I was baffled and realized I had to learn how this worked so I could instruct her.

Someone told me that a local college had a course on computers. I decided to get information by going to college myself. The name of the school was Keiser College, and I felt silly, a dumb person entering a college to inquire about taking a course. But I remember what Father Jim had said and walked in with my head held high.

Keiser College was a small local school back in 1990. It was not the large state university it is today, but it seemed huge to me when I walked in for the first time. What was I doing there? I was just about to walk out the door when an attractive young woman asked if she could help. I didn't know what to say, so I asked her where the restroom was. She politely showed me to the bathroom and said she would wait here for me, and she sat on a chair in the hallway. I don't remember how long I stayed in the restroom.

A young man entered and asked if I was all right. "Mrs. Morley ask me to check up on you. She is waiting in the hall for you"

I had to leave the restroom now. Mrs. Morley was probably wondering who I was. Indeed, I wasn't a student of my age. Perhaps I had a child in that school? I had to face her before she called 911 on me.

Out I came with a big smile on my face. "Hello, Mrs. Morley! My name is Bill Flynn, and Father Jim sent me. I mean, I want to inquire about working on computers."

"Are you looking for a job?" she asked.

"No. I would like to learn about computers," I said.

"Come with me to my office, and we can talk this over. I will need some information to get you started." Noticing my advanced age, she asked me why I was interested in computers. I told her about my granddaughter, and she smiled and said okay. "First, you have to take an exam for the course. It is a ten-week course that involves you coming two nights a week. Can you commit to that?"

I felt she was politely trying to push me off, but I said yes, thinking the entrance exam would end it all. No way was I about to pass an exam to enter college.

She explained to me the cost of the course and handed me a bunch of paperwork to fill out.

Then came the entrance exam, which was three pages of questions, one of them entirely mathematical. I had thirty minutes to complete the test. I figured I would be done in five and be on my way home. As I started, I began to think, Put some trust in Father Jim and try your best to answer the questions. What have you got to lose? Only a computer. I spent the whole thirty minutes giving the best answers I could. After the test, I went back to the hall to wait for the results. It was the most extended ten minutes of my life. How embarrassing it would be if she told me I wasn't accepted because I only answered one correct question.

Finally, Mrs. Morley called me in. This time, there was a man with her. "William, this is Mr. Art Keiser. He is the president of the college, and we would like to welcome you to Keiser College. You aced the exam."

Aced the exam? What were they telling me? I started to think this was a scam to get my money to take the course and flunk out.

"Your high score allows you to enroll in a class in biomedical engineering with financial aid from the college and student loans."

"Do you have the right test results?" I asked. "My name is William Dummy Flynn."

I went home, dumbfounded to talk this over with Jackie, who was of no help. We had been married now for twenty-five years, and this was probably the dumbest thing I ever said to her. Naturally, Father Jim would say, "Go for it, Professor."

Jackie had nothing to say about this, mainly because she didn't know what to say. Perhaps she was thinking, Let him have his dream. It won't last long. Well, if you are going to dream, why not dream in technicolor? But a biomedical engineer, what's that? I thought an engineer had something to do with trains. But when I was in college, the subject didn't matter. When I told my friends I was now in college, they would ask me, "What are you majoring in?" I said it wasn't the military.

I started attending class and found out fast just what a biomedical engineer was and what was involved in becoming one. First, you had to become a medical assistant doing a year and a half of medical terminology combined with a year and a half of computer repair then a six-month internship at a local hospital.

What was I thinking? I couldn't even spell "engineer," but I wanted to make Father Jim proud.

College was fun at first (I meant the first day). I was probably the oldest person there, including the teachers. The kids treated me with respect. They even voted me president of the school council. My third-grade teacher would be proud of me.

Classes were hard. I had to write everything down to remember (ADD) and then try to recognize what I wrote. I would rise at four in the morning to study, work for eight hours a day, and attend three hours of classes twice a week.

The best thing that ever happened to me was when I got fired from work. I was working as an assistant manager in a liquor store with a manager who didn't particularly like me. Murray felt I was after his job, and he let me know it. He said it was stupid for me to go to college, I would never graduate, and if I did, no one would hire me because of my age. All Murray did was inspired me to succeed.

When I ask him for time off to attend class, he decided to end my employment. I was able to collect unemployment and attend college full-time.

The college liked having me around all the time and even offered me a job at the library. Think about it, an elementary school dropout working as an assistant librarian at a college. I had to look it up in a dictionary to learn how to spell "librarian." Thank you, Father Jim.

My mother had always said, "Hard work pays off." But I didn't think that applied toward me. Like studying, why work hard if you can get it the easy way? Mom was right. Hard work paid off. I worked very hard, and it showed in my grades. I not only received passing grades but also high passing grades. I loved what I was accomplishing.

Time went fast, and I was about to start my internship when they called me to the councilors. "Mr. Flynn, you can't graduate! You don't have a high school diploma. You have to take a GED as soon as possible." Having received my general equivalency diploma (GED), I got qualified to start my six-month internship at a local hospital. Catholic nuns administrated the Holy Cross Hospital in Fort Lauderdale, Florida, and I was the first student to be accepted as an intern from my college.

I can't describe the pleasure I had experienced while at the Holy Cross Hospital. The manager of the biomed department was named Rich, and he was so friendly and helpful. Keiser had prepared me well, and I never stopped impressing Rich with my knowledge and work.

Six months went by quickly, and it was time for graduation commencement. What excitement and joy that day brought. All of my family were present, including my mother and sister, and a special surprise: Rich. I had the honor of leading the Pledge to the Flag and introducing the guest speaker.

When the time to hand out the diplomas and certificates, I was amazed at how many rewards I received: a certificate of honor for the honor roll and student council plus verbal praise for my work and attitude with the other students. While all this was going on, Rich was taking it all in, thinking that if he hired me, it would be like getting the first-round pick in the NFL. His graduation gift to me was a full-time job at the hospital. Thank you, Father Jim.

Working at the Holy Cross Hospital was indeed a pleasure. I was never treated this way before in my life. They treated me with respect like I was professional with dignity. I was involved in a conversation with doctors and nurses. I listened to them, and they worked with me. It was unbelievable. I couldn't wait to go to work every day. I was extremely happy, and it showed in my work.

My manager and now friend, Rich, decided to send me to school in New Jersey to study the datascope balloon pump. The classes were hard, and we had to know the pump inside and out, take it apart, and put it back together again. We needed to learn the therapy and how it worked. It is an important device that can save many lives when a heart does not have enough oxygen due to blocked coronary arteries. It must work harder to provide oxygen to the body. The pump helps to restore the balance between supply and demand for the oxygen needed for the heart and other organs to function correctly.

When I returned to the hospital, I was in charge of four pumps. That meant I had to share a workshop on the surgical floor. The man I shared the workshop was named Randy, and he was a well-experienced engineer who was able to teach me a lot. We became good friends, and we made working at the hospital even happier. Finally, my life was terrific! It couldn't be any better.

I decided to continue my education; and since Keiser, at that time, only offered an associate program, I would have to attend a university. My manager at the Holy Cross would provide the free hours from my schedule so I could attend classes and would even pay for them if I mainlined a certain grade point average.

I applied at Barry University and was accepted.

Booker T. Washington had once said, "I have learned that success is to be measured *not* so much by the position that one has reached in life as by the obstacles he has overcome while trying to succeed."

Chapter 2

Heart Problems

Heart attacks are a common occurrence today. We hear about them all the time. John had a heart attack. Sue had a heart attack. And for a moment, we feel sorry for them. We even say we will pray for them, but we don't. We don't think about them until they happen to a loved one or even yourself. The world of success as I know it came completely down on me by a series of heart attacks.

My first attack took place in May 1994. I was sitting in my living room couch while my wife, Jackie, and daughter Ginger were at the pool. All of a sudden, I started to feel sharp, aching radiation down my left arm. I was confused, not knowing what was happening. The last thing in my mind was I would have a heart attack. Then came the chest pain. I felt my chest was about to break into two. The pain was so severe that I couldn't move, even to get up from the couch to reach the telephone to call for help. I was in terrible shape and in big trouble.

Just then, Ginger came back from the pool; and with one look at me, she knew I was in trouble. All I could manage to say was "Get your mother." Looking back on it now, Ginger had probably saved my life.

Now there I was, sitting on the couch, surrounded by three paramedics poking at me. Although I could see them, I could not understand just what they were saying. They must have given me some nitroglycerin because I started to feel my chest loosening up, but I still could not understand what they were saying. One of them came closer and, with a loud voice, told me I was going to the hospital because I had a heart attack.

Wait a minute! I was too young to be having a heart attack, and I had a lot of work to do in my new job.

The next thing I knew, I was in the trauma room of the hospital, facing a stranger staring at me with a little boy by his side. I didn't have the strength to say anything, and I looked at him looking at me. Then I noticed I was not in a prone position but strapped to a board, standing up. Now that's strange.

Finally, the stranger spoke, "My name is Dr. Toto. Don't worry, you are in good hands, and you will be all right." He was right. About four hours later, I was alert and feeling better—confused and worried but feeling better.

Now Dr. Andrew Toto would play an essential part in my life for the next ten years. As a matter of fact, if it were not for Dr. Toto, I would probably not be here at all. Dr. Toto treated me for the next ten years with my eight heart attacks. But let's get back to the first one. After a week and a half in the hospital and another two weeks at home, I was able to return to work.

Being back to work was terrific. Thank God, it was a mild attack, and I was back so soon. But it didn't last long before the second attack came.

Jackie and I loved horses, and when we lived in Pembroke Pines, Florida, we found out about a horse time-share. A local ranch had about fifteen horses. As a member, all we had to do was call and request a horse, and it was made available for us. I liked a specific horse named Paladin (Fighter) who was fifteen hands high or about sixty inches, a color of bronze, and very shiny. He was an old horse of eight years or older but was very gentle and a joy to ride on. One day, while riding this champion, I started to feel that sharp, aching radiation down my left arm again, and I knew I was in trouble. I didn't know what to do. Jackie was way ahead of me, enjoying her ride; and here I was, a long way from the barn. I decided to let go of the reins, sit up on the stirrups, and hold on tight to the horn of the saddle. Paladin must have realized something was wrong and strolled straight back to the barn. To my surprise, Jackie was already at the barn, watching with a worried look on her face because of how Paladin was approaching. Once she was able to see the pain in my face, she immediately got me into the car and drove three blocks to the hospital. I was able to walk myself into the emergency room with my cowboy boots on and a swaggering walk like John Wayne.

Once again, I was looking at the face of Dr. Toto, but this time, I was in a bed and not strapped to a board. He said this one was a little more serious than the last and that a cauterization would show if I needed coronary bypass surgery.

The cauterization did show that I needed the surgery. Unfortunately, Dr. Toto was not qualified to perform the bypass and had to transfer me to a different hospital and another doctor. Believing I would have the surgery the same day, Dr. Toto decided to leave in me the narrow tube and called a catheter then inserted it into a blood vessel in my leg, so I had to lay flat as to not remove the catheter.

When I arrived at the hospital, they were waiting for me, and I immediately went to the operating room. Dr. Peck was to do the surgery. However, since I still had the tube inserted in me, he decided to do another cauterization and believed I didn't need the bypass and sent me back to Dr. Toto. I felt Dr. Toto was angry about this, but he would not say anything wrong about another doctor. He loaded me up with medicine and after several days and sent me home.

I returned to work, which lasted only two days, when my manager told me I needed a letter from my doctor before I could return to work. I was shocked when Dr. Toto said to me that I couldn't go back to work and handed me paperwork to apply for social security disability.

I was devastated. How could this be? I lived about three blocks from the hospital, so I walked home. But I was agitated and walked around the neighborhood about eight times under the hot sun, hoping I would have a heart attack and die. How could this be? My life was so good. I had graduated from college and had landed on a great job. How could I tell Jackie I was now out of work and out of luck? I was so worried and angry about my future that I started yelling at

God, "How can you do this to me?" I was so mad at him. It was like he was playing a game with me. He changed my life around, only to put me down. I had no choice but to apply for social security disability. It took me two years to get it.

The next several years were miserable. I was in and out of the hospital with heart problems. Finally, Dr. Toto had, had it. He wanted me in the Miami Heart Hospital and made arrangements to transfer me by ambulance. He and my wife, Jackie, would be there when I arrived.

The ambulance driver was very young, and I believed he was new to the job. The first clue was when he started to run out of gas and asked me if I had any money. I knew he wasn't kidding, and I began to worry. He had to turn back to a gas station his company had an account with and filled the gas tank, and off we went again.

The second clue was, it took a long time to Miami. I started to get the impression that something was wrong, and the stress was not good for my heart. Finally, he pulled up to the hospital and went in with the paperwork and came out quickly. We were at the wrong hospital.

When we arrived at the right hospital, Dr. Toto had an angry look on his face, and Jackie had a worried look. But neither said anything to the driver. They just rushed to the cauterization room and prepared me for the procedure, which Dr. Toto performed himself.

The results were not good. It revealed I had several blocked arteries in my heart, preventing blood flow to my heart. Dr. Toto told me my left main artery was blocked and that it was a vital artery that supplied most of the blood to the left ventricle. He continued that two other arteries were also severely blocked and that I would need atherosclerosis surgery. Looking at the confused look on my face, he said, "Bypass surgery." He also felt I was not in an emergency and that I could go home while he made arrangements. He wanted me to have the surgery at Mount Sinai Medical Center and the Miami Heart Institute. He also wanted a specific doctor to operate. His name was Dr. Williams (I am unable to remember his first name).

Two days later, I had the operation, and it went smoothly. I was operated on a Wednesday and felt good enough to go home on

Thursday. Dr. Williams was amazed at my success and even asked me to visit other patients who also just had a bypass and were not doing as well.

The only difficulty I experienced was my roommate. I can't tell you his name because he was from Cuba, and the single word in English he knew was "baseball." He would watch a whole nine innings standing directly in front of the television, and he would never sit down. But the real problem was, he would pull out all the tubes and IV that was attached to him and start walking down the hallway, bleeding all over the place. My wife was afraid he might pull out my tubes, but he didn't, and he even gave me a big hug when I was going home.

The surgery was in March 1995, and most of that year went uneventful, except for several trips to the emergency room due to arrhythmia and angina, which developed after the surgery. Both diseases needed to be taken seriously and treated. Fortunately, most of the trips to the emergency were false alarms but necessary.

December 14 of that year was the worst day of my life. My dearest mother went home to the Lord. She passed instantly from a blood clot in the leg (deep vein thrombosis or DVT) that traveled to her heart. It was a comfort knowing death came immediately and that she didn't suffer. The suffering was for my sister, Barbie, who discovered her lying on her bed.

I was devastated when I received the news. I felt so weak that I fell to the floor in shock. Again, Jackie and Ginger were with me. Ginger asked if she should call 911 to which Jackie said no. All they could do was comfort me.

The funeral was to be in Tampa, which meant we had to travel across the state. But before that, I had to get the approval of Dr. Toto, who was uneasy about the situation and advised that they keep a close eye on me. And he was right.

The trip to Tampa was the longest ever, and when we arrived at the cemetery, that familiar feeling in my chest started. Luckily, my brother-in-law, Lynn (Barbie's husband), alerted the funeral director of my condition. I felt I was about to start crying, so I went into the men's room and sat in one of the stalls. When I tried to get up, it was like my first heart attack on the couch, and I could not get up. Lynn was outside the stall and asked if I was all right. I was unable to answer. The next thing I realized was, I was in a Tampa hospital.

I had missed the funeral completely, which turned out to be a good thing. I never saw my mother in the casket. However, while in the hospital, someone I can't remember gave me a beautiful yellow rose from the funeral. It was a beautiful thing to do. But whenever someone entered the room, they admired the flower and asked me about it, and every time, would I start to choke up. After about a week and still in the hospital, I began to wonder if we would be home for Christmas. They still had several tests planned for me.

One day, my favorite brother-in-law, Lynn, arrived in my room with a probable CD player and some Bob Dylan CDs. Lynn was a huge Bob Dylan fan. Once Lynn had left, I decided to listen to the CD when all at once, I heard "Code Blue Room 211." Wait a minute! That's my room. All of a sudden, the doctors arrived, and the nurses with a crash cart were ready to shock me with the defibrillator when they noticed the CD player. The player was affecting the EKG leads in my chest. Sorry, no Bob Dylan.

One day, they told me I was going home, only to be determined by another doctor that it was not possible. More tests were needed.

Finally, I was discharged with no real explanation as to why I had to stay so long, only that I should see my cardiologist as soon as I got home. My sister suggested I remain perhaps for another week to rest and recuperate. But both Jackie and I wanted to be back for Christmas, and we arrived home on the twenty-third. Besides, it would be great to be on my own bed again.

The next few months were miserable. Losing my mother struck me hard. She was a special person and a wonderful mother. It took me a long time to accept the fact that she was gone. I am looking forward to seeing her again in heaven (if I get there). Her passing had started me to seriously think about God and heaven, realizing now both my parents went home with the Lord and that I was the next in line.

Here I was, fifty years old and in poor health and no real future. I had been angry with God for about a year now, and something didn't feel right. So I decided to talk to him again and give him another chance.

I had mentioned that the next few months were miserable. Well, actually, the next ten years weren't that great. My health continued to deteriorate. There were many trips to the emergency room. Besides angina and arrhythmia, I developed type 2 diabetes. With that came nephropathy (nerve damage and kidney damage). I lost the feeling in both feet and most of my legs.

Dr. Toto wanted me in a wheelchair, and I was able to get an electric one.

I felt useless and a burden for Jackie and my family. We went everywhere to the doctors or to visit other families. Jackie had to take the wheelchair apart to put it in the trunk.

We went on vacations, long trip, by car, and even on cruises. I tried to hide my pain. I believed I was successful at this most of the time. If she knew how much pain I was in, she was good at letting me hide it.

On my journey back to Jesus, I started reading books on the lives of saints. I was particularly fond of Padre Pio, also known as St. Pio of Pietrelcina. I was astonished as I read the saint's life and popularity, his spirituality and generosity to those in need, his peculiarity, and his sincere devotion to Mary, the Mother of Jesus. He was also a mystic with the ability to read hearts. But most importantly, he was famous for exhibiting the stigmata, the wounds of Jesus.

I read everything about Padre Pio that I could get my hands on. I read book after book, learning as much as I could and trying to imitate this great saint. I learned he displayed a great devotion to the Rosary, and that was my answer. I could never be a mystic or have the ability to read hearts and indeed not receive the stigmata, but I can be more generous and be more devoted to the Rosary. I started saying the Rosary every day and felt I was gaining a closer relationship with our Blessed Mother. Then I read somewhere (probably St. Louis de Montfort) that I prayed the Rosary in, say, a group of fifty people, I would receive credit for fifty Rosaries.

I was delighted when in the year 2000, we moved from Fort Lauderdale area to Stuart, Florida, about thirty-five miles north of

West Palm Beach and found a storefront parish called St. Andrews Catholic Church that had a priest who was devoted to both Padre Pio and our Blessed Mother Mary. I quickly became friends with Al and Anna Angline, two parish members who would drive me to the church every day so I could join the others in praying the Rosary.

I hope there is a heavenly accountant who is keeping tabs on my Rosary credits.

As I continued praying the Rosary, I felt I was getting closer to our Blessed Mother. The more I prayed, the more I wanted to pray. I thought this was good because I wanted to know Jesus more. I remember when I was a kid when I met a new friend, and in wanting to keep that friendship, I first had to make a good impression on his mother. I felt it was the same way with Jesus. If I made a good impression on Mary, she would lead me to her Son. And I was right! I prayed and prayed and prayed and knew I was making a good impression on Mary. I had a picture of her, and when I looked at it, she always smiled at me.

My prayers were like a rotten apple, all turning brown with holes in it and worms coming out of the holes. But Mary would take that apple and remove the pits and shine it like a bright-red diamond and present it to her Son.

I felt great. I was attending daily mass with holy people. I was around the right people, doing the right things, and getting to know Jesus better. A priest told me to offer my pain and suffering to the Lord so he could use it to help others. He must have helped a lot of people because I had a lot of pain and suffering.

Things were great. I had a good relationship with the Blessed Mother and was in partnership with her Son on helping other people with my pain and suffering. Over time, I felt my suffering was like a merchandise; the more I had, the more I had to offer. I wasn't useless anymore, and I was getting closer and closer to the Lord.

One day, during Mass, Father Jack, the priest, mentioned a place called Medjugorje where our Blessed Mother Mary was appearing to some children every day since 1981. I was very upset to hear this. What was he talking about? And how come I never knew about it? I needed to talk with him and straighten him out. When I finally met with Father Jack, he was persuasive, and I held back my professional advice. He gave me a book to read that would explain in detail what he was saying. I wasn't convinced and had no intention of reading the book. Why waste my time? But in respect to him as a priest, I told him I would. When I returned home, I threw the book on an end table, and that was the end of it.

Over the next few days, I couldn't stop staring at the book and the beautiful picture of Our Lady on the cover. It was as if she was telling me to read the book. Well, as always, I obeyed her and was mesmerized with what I was reading. The author claimed that back on June 24, 1981, Our Lady started appearing to some children under the title Our Lady of Medjugorje.

As I first started to read the book, I was doubtful. This was just probably a book by an author trying to sell another false story about the Catholic Church; after all, he was not even a Catholic. But for some reason couldn't put the darned book down. The more I read, the more I wanted to learn. It was like I was being guided by Our Lady or the Holy Spirit to read this book, and when I finished reading it, I developed a strong desire to read and learn more about Our Lady of Medjugorje. For the longest time, I couldn't even pronounce or spell it. It seemed I was reading everything I could get my hands on about this small town in Bosnia and Herzegovina in what was Yugoslavia, now referred to as Croatia.

Several months later, Father Jack mentioned he was planning a pilgrimage to Medjugorje and that there were still spots open to join him. I wanted to go!

My going to Europe was an impossibility in my condition. It would be a miserable trip for Jackie pushing me around in the chair. That was if she wanted to go. But I still could not get it out of my system, and I wanted to go! I felt like Our Lady was calling me to go, and I had to give her an answer. I decided to talk to Father Jack to see if it was possible for me to join the trip, and he said, "Yes. Someone will push you in the wheelchair. You will not be able to go up the mountain, but you can stay in the church and pray for those who do." His words stayed with me, and the more I was thinking about it, the more I wanted to go!

It was time now for me to discuss this with Jackie to see where she stood on this. That night, at dinner, I asked her, "How would you like to go to Medjugorje?"

She said, "Where?"

I said, "Medjugorje, the place where Father Jack said Our Lady is appearing someplace in Europe."

She laughed at me and said, "You're lucky you can go to Walmart."

I let it go at that.

Several weeks later, Father Jack announced he extended the trip to include Rome and Pietrelcina, the birthplace of Padre Pio, besides a trip to San Giovanni Rotondo where he spent over fifty years in the Capuchin Friary. That was all I needed to know, I have been praying to Padre Pio (my favorite saint) for years and never considered the possibility that I would ever have the opportunity like this. I was going!

I was so excited. How could Jackie say no to this? But she did. She had no interest in going and hoped it would be the end of it. But to her surprise, I said, "Okay, I'll go myself." She couldn't believe I would go. I made a firm comment to make this trip. I wrote out a check for the deposit and put it in the mailbox. Now there was no turning back. I was going to Medjugorje, wherever that was.

It was August 21, 2004, and I was unable to sleep, thinking about all I had to do before this trip, which was only four weeks away. I needed a passport and to know what to bring with me. I was on tons of medicine, would I need letters from doctors, and I was having second thoughts about going without Jackie. What was I thinking, traveling across the world in my condition by myself? I knew there would be plenty of members of the parish on this trip, including Father Jack, but it would not be the same without Jackie. We were hardly ever separated. I felt I was making a big mistake. The Croatian Mir Center in Miami was presenting the trip. I wanted to call them to get my deposit back. I still had this strong feeling Our Lady was calling me to go.

For most of the night, I was going back and forth in my mind, Should I go or not? After all, it was a lot of money, and going to

Rome was a trip of a lifetime. And here I was, going without Jackie. I started to feel very selfish. As I thought about the negative aspects of the trip, my thoughts were troublesome; however, when I concentrated on the thought that Our Lady was calling me, my mind was relaxed and peaceful. So I tried to think only of her. Still trying to go to sleep, I started to notice some strange feelings throughout my whole body, and I began to panic. Was I having another heart attack? Was this our Lord's way of telling me not to go? But this didn't feel right like the other heart attacks I had—no pain running down my left arm or in the middle of my chest, just a tingling feeling throughout my whole body like when your foot falls asleep.

It was 2:00 a.m. I felt the need to use the bathroom, so I got up and walked into the bathroom. Let me repeat that: I got up and walked into the bathroom. I realized I didn't need my cane or had to hold onto the wall. I could feel a new strength in my body, and I just sat on my bed. After a short period, everything went away. I was feeling nothing at all—no strange things anymore and no pain. Wait a minute! With no pain, no nerve damage pain from nephropathy, and no chest discomfort, I could feel my toes for the first time in years. I thought about this for hours. What happened? And was I still dreaming? How could I tell Jackie?

Just as I was about to yell for Jackie, "Help me, I am dying!" a new calmness came over me. Was I sleeping? Was this just a dream? I was now enjoying this warm feeling throughout my body. It was like the feeling you get if you ever have a cauterization and they shoot the dye into your veins. I didn't want the mood to go away. If this was dying, bring it on.

I decided to wake her up slowly, very slowly. When she was fully awake, my mouth couldn't work. I couldn't say a word, so I started to move around like I was dancing. She got the message. Now when you had eight heart attacks and a stroke, you are more or less on speed dial with your cardiologist, so Jackie called Dr. Toto immediately and told him I was in the living room, jumping up and down, claiming I had healing or something like that. Poor Jackie, she never understood what had happened, and neither did I.

Dr. Toto told her to be in his office first thing in the morning. The next day, in his office, he was able to take every kind of test he could, including a stress test. After all the tests, he told me my heart hadn't sounded this good in ten years. Now that was something to wonder about because it had been almost exactly ten years since my first heart attack.

We left his office as bewildered as when we came in. It was a very silent ride home. We didn't know what to say. For the next several days, I tried to digest just what was going on with me and came up with no answers. Was it possible Our Lady had healed me for the trip? No, that was foolish. I didn't have that great of a relationship with her. I was mostly going on the trip because of Padre Pio. Besides, I believed only her Son, Jesus, could heal someone.

I decided not to tell anyone of this, mostly because I didn't know what to say. How could I explain to someone something I didn't understand myself? I could wait until God would send me an instruction book.

In the parish, there was a new administrant by the name Ed, a big man with an easygoing manner who was a delight to talk with, the perfect person for the job. Ed Kelly was his full name. In the past, Ed had traveled to Medjugorje several times, so he was the ideal person to ask questions concerning the trip. He was accommodating and patient and encouraging in answering my questions. It was evident Ed believed that Our Lady also challenged him to come to her mountain and to a complete renunciation of his former ways. Since then, Ed had written several books on his Medjugorje experiences. Again, he was accommodating and seemed sincerely happy that I was joining him on his next trip. It also appeared I had made a new friend.

He also told me a little about the woman named Maria who would be the tour guide and how it took a little time to get used to. He described her as a woman with a deep husky voice and X-ray eyes that looked right through you. But she was a woman of prayer and that I would learn like her, and I did.

In addition to the functional aspects of the trip, Ed also pointed out some of the unfortunate but necessary elements, such as the twenty or so hours it would take to travel to Rome, the hassle of airline transfers and connections, not to mention the anguish of going through customs. But all this would be forgotten once we would arrive at Medjugorje.

I was still confused and concerned about what had occurred in my life. There could be no explanation as to what had happened and that I would be laughed at by anyone whom I would tell about it. Why couldn't Jackie and I talk about it? I certainly could not tell my new friend, Ed.

I appreciated that Ed took the time for me and helped me build up my confidence, and now I felt better about going; however, I still had some anguishes about going without Jackie.

The long-awaited day finally arrived when Jackie was to drive me to the airport. Jackie continued asking me during the drive if I remembered to take this or that. We had never been separated like this before. We had always spent vacations together, and now I would be traveling across the world to places unknown to us. Still not understanding my healing, she was probably worried about my health. "Do you have all your medicines?"

I was heartbroken when she drove off in the car without me. All the guilt feelings came back. Why was I doing this without her? How could I justify spending so much money on myself? But this was not a vacation; it was a pilgrim's journey. And besides, Our Lady was calling me, and I had to answer.

Once inside the airport, everything went smoothly. There were no problems checking in at the international ticket counter and at the departing gate. I recognized several parishioners from St. Andrews, including Ed Kelley and his wife, Jean; Jack Telnack and his wife, Marguerite; and Joe and Sharon Duyon. They all welcomed me on the trip, and Ed introduced me to the others.

I was alone my first trip to Europe. Thankfully, Ed took me, as they say, under his wing and made me feel comfortable. There were nine of us from the parish, and a little later, a group from somewhere out west arrived to join the trip.

One noticeable absent person was Father Jack, who was nowhere in sight. I wondered about this but didn't say a word. He was one of my reasons for going, and now where was he? However, I did notice another priest talking to Ed. He motioned over to meet Father Chuck, whom Ed called the Good Shepherd. Father Charles Notabartolo held a high position in the diocese as vicar general and moderator of the curia. At that time, I had no idea what the titles meant, except that he must have held a significant position in the diocesan administration. And now he was traveling with us. That added more pressure. But Father Chuck proved to be one of the most personable, down-to-earth persons I had ever meet. Ed was correct in calling him the Good Shepherd. He stayed with the group throughout the whole pilgrimage, explaining what we didn't understand, hearing confessions and, in general, was being a great spiritual adviser. He was a priest you would feel comfortable talking to in spite of his position, a good chaplain for us on this pilgrim's journey—and yes, a good shepherd.

Father Chuck had received a phone call that Father Jack would be unable to join the trip because he was in the hospital. No more information was given as to the reason why.

The overnight flight was long and tedious—thirteen hours of trying to sleep with no success. Staying in one area for that long was very hard; but we, on our way to Rome, were too excited to sleep.

We arrived in Rome around 10:00 a.m., which confused me because of the six-hour time difference. I was exhausted. I didn't care if it was Rome or Miami! I just wanted to get some sleep.

The customs lines were very long but moved quickly and without a hitch. Once in the airport, we were met by this husky-voiced little woman whom Ed had described to me. She lined us up like we were about to face a firing squad, spitting out commands and orders that would put a marine drill instructor to shame. I named her the Crazy Croatian. She herded us into a bus that was driven by her cousin. As we headed toward the heart of Rome, we all became alert and forgot about sleeping. I couldn't believe we were driving down the streets of Rome. All the sites were amazing—the buildings, the people, and all the motorcycles and little cars. It seemed that parking would be a problem in this ancient city.

It was different, and it was beautiful.

At the hotel, we enjoyed a nice dinner, and some sleep until 6:00 a.m., the time we would depart for Assisi. In this beautiful village, I discovered one of the greatest saints who ever lived: St. Francis of Assisi. Little did I know at that time what a significant influence St. Francis would have on me for the rest of my life.

The very next day, we were on the cousin's bus, headed for San Giovanni Rotondo. The town was renowned for being the home of St. Pio of Pietrelcina from July 28, 1916, until his death on September 23, 1968. How thrilling it was for me to walk in the footprints of my favorite saint, to touch the things he might have felt, and to see the room he had lived and died. I could have stayed there forever, but the cousin's bus was headed back to Rome that same day. I would have to return here again, and I did twice and with Jackie.

Back in Rome, we visited all the shrines we could, including a general audience with Pope John Paul II. We did this in only two days. My new friend, Ed, being a big man with a big heart and always helping others, was pushing a man in a wheelchair all around Rome. For his reward, while at the pope's audience, Ed was ushered to bring the wheelchair onto the platform next to the pope and, afterward, was paraded in front of the pope to shake his hand. Perhaps I should have stayed in a wheelchair.

Now we were finally on our way to Medjugorje. From the Roman airport, we traveled via Croatian Airlines to a town called Split and then a two-hour-forty-five-minute bus ride across the mountains to reach Medjugorje, located in the Herzegovina region of Bosnia and Herzegovina. I was quite nervous because the mountain roads were narrow and at times hanged over cliffs. The driver appeared to be a professional who had driven this route many times. However, I was amazed at how he could keep the bus on the road. Maria wasn't concerned at all, but I was greatly relieved when we hit solid ground.

Throughout the entire trip, Maria stood at the front of the bus, telling in great detail the history of Medjugorje and the apparitions.

It was on June 24, 1981, the Feast of St. John the Baptist, when six visionaries first saw our Lady.

Ivanka Ivankovic-Elez was the first to see Our Lady on July 21, 1966. Ivankovic-Mijatovic was the oldest of the visionaries as she was born on September 3, 1964.

Ivan Dragicevic Ivan was the oldest of the two boys. He was born on May 25, 1965.

Mirjana Dragicevic-Soldo Mirjana was born on March 18, 1965.

Marija Pavlovic-Lunetti Marija was the third oldest of the visionaries. She was born on April 1, 1965.

Jakov Colo was the youngest of them. He was born on March 6, 1971.

Our Lady wants to lead us to a living and profound encounter with Christ and to show the world a path to peace. Our Lady gave messages in her apparitions, which she was to pass on to the general public. Although there were many messages, they can be grouped under five topics because all messages lead to or illustrate these five topics: peace, faith, change, prayer, and fasting. The apparitions continue even today. However, Our Lady had told the children that she would give them ten secrets. Very little is known about these secrets, though we do know that some of them have to do with chastisements for the world. We also know that the third secret will be a visible, lasting sign that will miraculously be placed somewhere on Apparition Hill. It will be permanent, durable, and beautiful. She had also said that once they received all ten secrets, she would no longer appear to them daily.

To date, only three visionaries—Mirjana, Ivanka, and Jakov—had received all ten secrets and could no longer see Our Lady daily. Mirjana received the tenth secret on December 25, 1982, and Our Lady promised to appear to her on March 18 for the rest of her life. Ivanka received the tenth secret on May 6, 1985, and her last daily apparition was the following day, May 7, 1985. Our Lady told her that she would appear to her on June 25 for the rest of her life.

Jakov received the tenth secret on September 12, 1998. Our Lady promised Jakov that he would have annual apparitions every December 25, Christmas Day.

As I listened to Maria talk, I realized that this was not an ordinary tour guide. She spoke with such passion. She was not a crazy Croatian but a woman who solemnly loved what she was telling us. You could see it in her face and hear it in her words. All that I had ever been told or read about Medjugorje were true, and now I was closer to this spiritual village and Our Lady. With each mile closer, my joyousness intensified. I couldn't wait to arrive where Our Lady visits. But to arrive there, we had to cross Bosnia and Herzegovina's border. All of a sudden, things became very serious. Maria, with a stern look, told us to hold up our passports and keep our mouths shut. I lost all the good feelings I was having about Our Lady and started to worry. Was I about to spend the next fifty years in a Bosnian prison?

A mean-looking huge guard walked out of a building toward our bus, his hand on the gun attached to his belt. His eyes were grim, and his posture was serious. He looked like he didn't know the war was over or that he wanted to start a new one.

I was confused and alarmed. I had never experienced anything like this before.

The guard entered the bus and slowly walked up and down, his hand still on the gun, checking each person's passport and looking seriously at each person's face but never saying a word.

All we could do was stare at Maria, hoping that she was the only person who could save us. We remained remarkably silent.

The guard went to the front of the bus and asked Maria questions, which she answered in a commanding voice. The guard appeared to be satisfied and stepped off the bus. We continued on our way; however, I wondered how many of us had wanted the bus to turn around and head home.

The war I mentioned was the Croatian War of Independence fought from 1991 to 1995 between the Croatian forces and the Serb-controlled Yugoslav army. Croatia won the war, but you wouldn't know it by the sites we had seen as we drove deeper into Croatia. Small villages still had bombed-out buildings and roads.

Maria continued her talk. We all settled down, realizing that she had been through this many times. I felt very peaceful as she went on about her experiences with Medjugorje. She also informed us that we would be staying at the home of Jakov Colo, the youngest among the seers. I began to wonder if he had a huge house.

Once we finally arrived at the small spiritual village, I was much relieved and exhausted. All I wanted to do was find a bed and sleep for hours. But that was not to be with Maria. After all, this was not a vacation. It was a pilgrimage, and every minute counted.

Arriving at Jakov's home, I was surprised to be greeted by a thirty-three-year-old man and not the young boy. Everything about him had taken place when he was about ten. He now had a wife and three children. Jakov greeted us as the bus pulled up in his broken English. I found him to be very friendly, and I felt sincerely welcomed.

His house was of average size, which he and his father had built themselves to accommodate the guests. Maria had added to the back of the house rooms that could provide for the pilgrims, including a large room that served as a dining room. During the evenings, Maria and Jakov would hold sessions where Jakov would speak to us about Our Lady. We were able to ask questions through Maria's interpretation.

We were all amazed at how he grew up in Our Lady's presence. Being only ten years old when Our Lady first appeared to him, and he still has apparitions, can anyone imagine an encounter with heaven and Our Lady and live in this corrupt world?

He told us how Our Lady urged him to pray, especially for the pilgrims and the sick. Another time, he asked what the Virgin expected of the Franciscans in Medjugorje. She answered, "Have them persevere in the faith and protect the faith of the people." Another time, he was concerned because the people were treating them like liars, and he wanted to know "how must we pray?" to which Our Lady answered, "My angels, do not be afraid of injustices. They have always existed. Continue to recite the Lord's Prayer, the Hail Mary, and the Glory Be God seven times. But also, add the Creed."

When asked about the ten secrets, he could only say very little. He revealed, "The Blessed Mother told all the visionaries that she would give ten secrets to them. The contents of these secrets remain hidden." To date, only three visionaries—Mirjana, Ivanka, and himself—had received all ten secrets and could no longer see Our Lady.

He received the tenth secret on September 12, 1998. Our Lady promised Jakov he would have annual apparitions every December 25, Christmas Day.

Jakov added,

> [1]On Friday, September 11th, during the regular apparition, Our Lady told me to prepare myself pecially by prayer for tomorrow's apparition because She will confide the 10th secret to me. On Saturday, September 12th, Our Lady came at 11:15 a.m. (local time). When She came, She greeted me as always with "Praised be Jesus." While She was confiding the 10th secret to me, She was sad. Then with a gentle smile, She said to me:

> "Dear child! I am your mother and I love you, unconditionally. From today I will not be appearing to you on Christmas, the birthday of my Son. Do not be sad, because as a mother, I will always be with you and like every true mother, I will never leave you. And continue further to follow the way of my Son, the way of peace and love and try to persevere in the mission that I have confided to you. Be an example of that man who has known God and God's love. Let people always see in you an example of how God acts on people and how God acts through them. I bless you with my motherly blessing and I thank you for having responded to my call."

He concluded by saying that the Blessed Virgin Mary had told the visionaries that the third secret would be a lasting sign placed on

---

[1] www.medjugorj.ws/en/messages/980912a/ Our Lady of Medjugorje message to Jakov Colo Sept. 12, 1998.

Apparition Hill. All six visionaries knew what they would be. They said that it will be a beautiful, durable, permanent sign and all those who go to Medjugorje will be able to see it.

I enjoyed listening to him and realized that I was in the presence of an extraordinary and most holy man. I could feel his sincerity, and indeed, Our Lady had called me here. As each day passed, I was conscious that my life was changing. I had no visions or heard any voices, but Our Lady had messages for me also, and they were coming in loud and clear. I believed she had a message for everyone who answered her call and came to Medjugorje. I knew at that moment I had to change my life and become the person Jesus had created me to be. But what was that?

Early one morning, just about the break of dawn with the sun shining in the window and on my face, I was unable to sleep, so I decided to get some fresh air. Outside the house, I was surprised to see another man standing in the driveway, for it was only about 5:30 a.m. Once the man noticed me, he came toward me with concern on his face, asking me if everything was all right. It was Jakov himself. I told him I was a light sleeper, and he said he also was a light sleeper and that he liked to come out early to feed the cats. As I looked around, I saw five stray cats, and we started talking about our love for cats (I had two at home). I had spoken to many important men in my life—cardinals, and bishops—but none were as important as one who had spoken to the Blessed Virgin. At first, I was very nervous and didn't know what to say, but he was amiable and made me feel comfortable after we talked about the cats. He asked me what part of Florida I lived. I told him, and he wanted to know how far that was from Miami. He said he was in Miami once. I noticed his broken English was much better on a one-on-one basis. I was delighted that our conversation was all small talk. I was afraid to ask him any questions.

He must have detected that and started asking about my family, names of my wife and children, their ages, and how long I was married. He told me that his wife was Italian, her name was Annalisa, and they were married on Easter Sunday in 1993 and now had three children: Arianna Marija, age nine; David Emmanuele, age eight; and Myriam, age five (remember, this was back in 2004).

Our little conversation ended when other pilgrims started to wake up and come down for breakfast. It was a brief talk with Jakov but one I would always remember. Imagine talking to man who talks to the Blessed Virgin.

During the day, Maria kept very busy climbing mountains and saying the Rosary. We started our days attending the 10:30 a.m. English mass at St. James where there could be as many as twenty priests on the altar at one time. The Franciscan priest was earnest about the mass. We would arrive half an hour early to say the Rosary and prepare for the mass. We had to be completely silent, and if there were any noise at all, a priest or brother would come to the microphone put his finger to his lip and say hush!

I had never been to a mass like this before; it was extraordinary mystifying. I was mesmerized and involved in the mass. The priest's words penetrated my ears and went straight to my heart. For the first time, I understood the mass. I felt like I left the earth and was attending Mass in heaven. I wished it would last forever, but it didn't, and I had to come back to reality. For the rest of the day, I thought about that feeling. Slowly, something in me was changing, and I had no idea. But it was mostly peaceful, and I could feel Our Lady's presence all around me.

One day, we went mountain climbing. Maria told us that this was Cross Mountain and that while climbing this mountain, we should reflect on our relationship with God and what we need to change in our lives to draw closer to him. Reflecting on this, I realized I had no real relationship with God. I only know of him, but I didn't know him. Things had to change! I had to change.

The name Medjugorje means "between mountains"—Cross Mountain and Apparition Hill. Our Lady had made it clear that she wanted pilgrims to climb both mountains, and Maria made sure that we did. At the base of Apparition Hill stood the Blue Cross that was placed to mark the spot where Our Lady appeared to the visionaries while they were being persecuted and hunted by the communist police in the early days of the apparitions. The area around the Blue

Cross is a place for quiet prayer and solitude, and over the years, many healings have been known to take place.

Krizevac means "Mount of the Cross." Also called Cross Mountain, is the highest mountain in the area and the most challenging to climb. The story of Cross Mountain goes that in 1933, the parishioners of St. James had wanted to erect a large cross on the top of the hill to commemorate the 19th anniversary of Jesus's Passion and death on the cross. The sixteen-ton cross, in which the parishioners, at a tremendous hardship, carried up all of the materials, was completed on March 15, 1934. The cross itself is a relic of the True Cross of Jesus that was received from Rome from Pope Pius X. Numerous healings have been known to take place at the summit of the mountain and at the foot of the cross after the pilgrims arrive at the top.

It was a challenging but a pleasurable experience climbing the mountain. I was amazed at seeing elderly people being carried on stretchers or in chairs or barefoot. But it was the faith of the people that was most impressive to see.

On August 30, 1984, Our Lady told the visionaries, "I love the cross, which you have providentially extraordinarily erected on Mount Krizevac. Go there more often and pray."

Pope Pius XI proclaimed 1933 a holy year because it marked the 1,900th anniversary of our Lord's death on the cross.

It was on this holy mountain that miracles happened, and several had happened to me. The first took place before we left Jakov's house. Being a diabetic, I had to use the restroom to urinate frequently. Knowing we would be on the mountain most of the morning, I believed it best to use the bathroom before we left. The odd thing was, I was unable to urinate as much as I tried, and I became very concerned. I couldn't stay in the bathroom much longer, or they might leave without me. Besides, someone else might need the room. I had to go now. The anxiety increased to a greater extent because I was told there were no restrooms on the mountain. I was now in a panic. Perhaps I should not climb and stay at the house. But Maria, in her usual controlling voice, said we all had to climb the mountain. No excuses! Well, that ended at that. I was going.

A fantastic thing took place for the three hours on the mountain: I had no desire or need to urinate.

The second occurrence took place when a girl named Barbara, one of the members of our group, told me, "Bill, your rosary beads have turned gold."

I told her it was impossible and that they were gold all the time.

She said, "No. The other day, after the Rosary, you were telling someone about them that they were your grandmother's and that you didn't know how old they were. I was admiring them from a distance, but I could clearly see that they were definitely silver."

I let it go. I didn't want to disagree with her, for she was very friendly. But I started to wonder if Maria was coming into our rooms at night with a can of spray paint. The first thing I asked Jackie when I got home was what color the beads were. She said silver. Now fifteen years later, they are still gold.

The third miracle took place at the top of the mountain. I was amazed at what I had seen—people of all ages circling the large cross, on their knees. It hurt me just to watch them. Someone told me that some would stay on their knees all day. What kind of faith was that? And why didn't I have it?

It would be impossible for me to describe the next and most significant phenomenon that happened in my life, one that would bring about a complete transformation and put it all together for me. It was called the the "miracle of the sun."

Chapter 3

The Miracle of the Sun

I was sitting and resting on a large rock, watching and being fascinated by what I was seeing on the top of the holy mountain. I had never felt this peaceful in my life. It was like I was taken from the earth and transported to a heavenly place. All turned silent as I sat, spellbound, watching these faithful people. I remember thinking, Did I die? Was this heaven? Great, I made it! My mind was clear. I couldn't think of anything, except Our Lady and how she chose these people and this little village to appear to. I didn't belong here, or did I?

I hear a loud voice, saying, "Look at the sun!" What, look at the sun? Are you crazy? You can't look at the sun.

As I looked around, everyone was staring directly at the sun. I was not about to. So far, on this trip, I was almost put in prison, had lost my hearing, and now I was about to go blind. I don't think so! But as I looked around, I could see my friend Ed and his wife, Jean, looking at the sun; and I remembered him telling me about this. Terrified to do this, I started to think of how Our Lady had gotten me this far and all the beautiful blessings I had received so far. Perhaps I should trust her complexity and do this.

I looked up at the sun, which seemed pale and did not hurt my eyes. Looking like a ball of snow, rotating on itself, it suddenly seemed to come down in a zigzag, appearing to be loosened from the sky and approaching the earth. It looked like a scarlet flame, and it turned yellow and deep purple. I fell to my knees and was incapable of moving. Tears flowed from my eyes, but I was not terrified anymore. I realized this was another gift I was receiving from Jesus. I became so relaxed and undisturbed by anything around me. I felt so much love in me for everything and everyone. The grass, the trees, and the people seemed so exquisite. This holy mountain was undoubtedly part of heaven, or as I heard, it was said that this was "the closest I would get to heaven on this earth." I didn't want to leave; I tried to keep this feeling forever.

We were only on the mountain for several hours, but it felt like a lifetime. My head was spinning and hurting at the same time trying to interpret all that was going on. It seemed that my whole life was revealed to me, and it wasn't pretty. This, I understood, is what takes place when you stand before the judgment seat, but I wasn't dead. I was fully alive. Was this real? Or was it just my imagination? I didn't tell anyone about this, not even my new friend, Ed. But it was something that I would meditate on for the rest of my life.

Coming down the mountain was as hard as climbing it, maybe even harder. All the way down, I kept repeating, "Lord, remember me when I enter your kingdom." It started to come altogether for me. I didn't have any visions or hear any voices, but I knew something or someone was communicating with me. I believed everyone here was having the same experience, but we were afraid and didn't know how to talk about it.

All my past sins were flowing in my mind. I could not remember any good memories. It was as if God was telling me what a wrongful person and just how smutty my soul really was. God was always standing next to me; he would never leave. But he couldn't penetrate my soul as long as I maintained this attitude of hate and unforgivingness. Many times, I would tell a person I forgive him or her and didn't mean it or told someone I would pray for them and didn't. Every time these words were spoken, God heard them.

Did you ever feel like there was someone else in the room with you but wasn't or hear a voice when you were alone? I believe it is your consciousness trying to tell you something. That is how God communicates with us. But most times, we don't recognize or don't want to know his voice. Understanding and accepting his words means we have to change the way we are living!

I was hearing his message loud and clear, but I liked my life the way it was. I was a nice person. A little venial sin couldn't hurt (yes, it can)! I attended Mass every Sunday (even sinners do that)! I went to confession regularly (even sinners do that).

Things had to change drastically. It was like I was given a second chance at life. But how to do this, I had no idea.

Once at home, Jackie was thrilled to see me, which felt strange since I was only gone for two weeks. She thought I wasn't coming back and that I joined a monastery somewhere in the mountains of Europe. I told her all that had happened on the trip, that she would have to go back with me to experience and understand precisely the change in me, and that if she didn't, we could never be on the same page spiritually. If she was unable to understand my healing, how would she know what had happened to me in Medjugorje when I didn't realize it myself?

My life now became hectic. Father Jack, knowing of my healing, said I had to visit the sick in the hospitals and nursing homes to share the gift I had received. He said, "God didn't give to you to stay at home, watching John Wayne movies. You have to share them with others." I didn't like this at first because I felt it would be putting all the attention on me and not our Blessed Mother. Besides, I was still waiting for an instruction book from Jesus. I was bewildered and too tired to do anything. But after much prayer, I decided to listen to Father Jack but did things slowly. I agreed to become a hospital minister.

Chapter 4

Saint Robert

Father Jack teamed me up with a very experienced minister, Robert De Roy, Bob as he was affectionately called. He appeared to be a silent kind of person, or maybe it was I was so nervous that I couldn't stop talking, and he couldn't get a word. He was a mild-mannered man, indeed a man of few words. But when he spoke, he was worth listening to.

Around that time (2005), Bob was around fifty-three years old, and I was sixty-two. He was much wiser. He was the type of person who felt good to be around. He was another blessing for me. He became my friend. Not only friends, we became brothers.

On our first day at the hospital, Bob instructed me on prayers to say for sick persons. I followed him to several rooms to observe how a hospital minister would conduct himself. I was amazed at his genteelness and compassion toward each patient. It showed he cared, and they could feel it too. I knew at once I was in the presence of a saint.

After visiting a few more rooms, Bob told me I would go to the next room myself. Inside was an older woman who was unresponsive and unable to receive the Host, and I should say a few prayers. What was this a joke? A test to see if I made the grade?

I entered the room. As I stood at the foot of the bed, silently praying and staring at her face, a strange and relaxing feeling came over me. I was not apprehensive at all. I felt great joy. As I looked at this poor elderly sick woman, I realized there was a connection between us. That connection was God, and we were related. God created her just like he created me, and God doesn't show favorites. He loves us all equally. That made her my sister, and I had to love her as he did. If I couldn't see God in her face, I couldn't see him on my own.

When I finished the prayers, I bent down and started whispering the Our Father in her ear. And as I spoke the words, I noticed a little smile on her lips; and when I finished and said amen, I could hear a weak, soft voice saying amen also. Was this real or just my imagination?

I left the room, shaking and almost in tears. Bob took hold of me and, with that beautiful smile, said it was the Holy Spirit working in me and added that I was a natural at this.

I became somewhat addicted to visiting the sick. I ended up going to five different nursing homes, the hospital, and some homebound. I couldn't get enough. To me, being around the sick was being with Jesus. I had a genuine love for them.

Did I mention Bob was a saint? Well, this was proof of it. One day, while at the hospital, I entered a room to find a woman crying. I pulled a chair next to her bed and asked, "Why are you crying?" She told me that she couldn't get ahold of her family in Guatemala to let them be aware that she was in the hospital because she had no money for a phone call. I told her I could not help her because I didn't carry cash and only had a debit card, but I was willing to go to St. Vincent de Paul when I finished my rounds. "They will help you," I said to the woman.

Now Bob and I had a habit of going to lunch after our visits to the hospital. I had finished visiting all the patients on my list and met with Bob, who asked, "Are we going to lunch?"

"Yes," I said, "but first, I have to go to St. Vincent de Paul."

He asked me the way, and I told him about the crying woman. He didn't say a word but took out his wallet and handed me all the money in it, saying, "Give this to her."

I was shocked at the amount of money he was giving her and asked him to come and meet the woman.

He said, "No, tell her that it came from St. Andrews and Father Jack." I knew that wasn't true, that it came from him. He ended by saying, "You probably will have to buy lunch."

Bob's friendship was a blessing and a gift for me. It was like my present priest, Fr. Aidan Hynes, was known to say frequently to get his point across, "God's gifts don't fall from the sky like the rain but from the people we meet." Father Hynes was right! The proof of this was Bob De Roy.

As time went on and we continued our ministry and friendship, our conversations became more like instructions.

I never told Bob of my healing, but he seemed to know all about me. Perhaps Father Jack told him, but we never discussed it. But he did, however, inquire about my education. When I told him about my history, he told me, "That was God working in you, preparing you for his plan for you."

Quoting the Bible, he said in 1 Corinthians 1:27–31 that God tells us he "chose the lowly and despised of the world, those who count for nothing, to reduce to nothing those who are something, so that no human being might boast."

Bob added that God had a plan for everyone, and that included me. He believed when God looked upon me, he knew I needed some help, and that's why I ended up in college at age fifty. It was not the college courses I was choosing but the path he selected for me. "After the proper education, he needed to teach you humility, and that was the heart attack." He had seen something in me that I had never seen in myself.

Bob taught me how to read the Bible as Catholics should: first, by praying to the Holy Spirit before reading and asking for guidance and understanding; and second, to put ourselves in the readings. He gave me this example from Matthew 27:21–24 when the crowd was calling for the crucifixion of Jesus. We had judge them too quickly. He claimed that if we were in that crowd, we would also call for his execution.

There is much more to reading the Bible. You have to place yourself in the period in which you are reading. If you are reading about Jerusalem, what was happening in Jerusalem during that period? How did the people live? What did they eat? How did they dress? If you don't understand the passage, look for other sources to help you. You must become a part of the Bible to understand it completely and to know what God is telling you.

"Remember," he would say, "what the Bible means.

B—basic
I—instructions
B—before
L—leaving
E—earth

Jesus is on every page of both New and Old Testaments."

Bob had two quotations he always cited: One, "It will all work out in the end, and if it does not work out, it's not the end." Second, "I don't know what the future holds, but I know who holds the future." Bob only had one weakness I know of, and that was chocolate chip cookies. He loved them but, for some reason, had to hide them from Carol.

Before I would visit Bob, I would first go to the bakery to buy some fresh, hot cookies, and we would stuff our faces during our conversations.

Carol volunteered at the Light for the World, an origination that collected medical equipment and medicine, along with doctors who also volunteered their time by visiting poor counties in South America. Her hours were her own, and I believed she had set her hours around my visits so we could eat the cookies. However, one day, she came home early, only to find the chocolate evidence all over our faces.

I once asked Bob as we were sitting in his library, admiring his collection of books on various subjects. "What made you decide to do this particular ministry?" I was talking about the hospital and homebound visits.

In his own instructive, friendly manner and that million-dollar smile, he said, "I already told you several times. Read the lives of the saints. Have another cookie, and I will explain it to you again." He reached up, almost without looking as if he knew where the book he wanted was, and pulled from the shelf one titled, *Butler's Lives of the Saints*. He turned to a page he had marked and to a section on St. Camillus de Lellis, the patron saint of the sick. He said, "The saints were, at one time, what we are now. And by imitating them can we become what they are." Turning back to the book, he read to me the writings concerning St. Camillus. He read out loud, "Camillus believed the holy charity was the root of all the virtues."

I asked why it read "holy charity" and not just "charity." What was holy charity?

He just smiled at me and said, "You have the *Catechism of the Catholic Church*. Look up the seven virtues, and you will find that it defines virtue as a 'habitual and firm disposition to do the good.'"

I asked him, "How do you remember all this?"

Again, he reached at the bookshelf and handed me the *Catechism*, and I opened it to where he had a marker on: "Article 7: The Virtues." It was as if he knew we would be having this conversation and was well prepared.

He asked me to read out loud section 1803, which I did. "Whatever is true, whatever is honorable, whatever is just, whatever is pure, whatever is lovely, whatever is gracious, if there is any excellence, if there is anything worthy of praise, think about these things."

"Stop there for a moment," Bob said. "Think about what you are reading. 'We must be truthful, honorable, just, pure, and gracious.' Who do we know is like this? Now read on, and think about what you are reading."

"A virtue is a habitual and firm disposition to do the good. It allows the person not only to perform good acts, but to give the best of himself. The virtuous person tends toward the good with all his sensory and spiritual powers. He pursues the good and chooses it in concrete actions. The goal of a virtuous life is to become like God. Philippians 4:8."

"This must be our goal," said Bob. "We must strive daily to achieve it. Let's talk about St. Camillus. He was on fire with the holy virtues, not only toward God but also toward his fellow man and especially toward the sick. Bob now read from the *Liturgy of the*

Hours. 'The mere sight of the sick was enough to soften and melt his heart and make him utterly forget all the pleasures and interest of this world.'" He went on to read, "'In the sick, he saw the person of Christ.' There it is, seeing the person of Christ in the sick that we visit. Put it this way. When you go to confession, you know you are not talking to a priest but to Jesus. It is the same when we visit the sick. We are visiting Jesus. We are fulfilling one of the seven virtues, holy charity."

He repeated that I read the *Lives of the Saints.* "Take the book home," he said. "You may keep it. It's a gift. Find a saint or two that you like, and imitate their virtues."

I truly enjoyed my time with Bob. He was a gift God had sent to me. Again, I remembered what Father Hynes had instilled in me, "God's gifts don't fall from the sky like the rain but comes to us from each other." I often wondered why it took God over sixty years to bring Bob into my life. They say God works in mysterious ways. I guess it was part of his plan for me that I would need Bob in this period of my life. When God gives you a job to do, he gives you the tools to do it, and Bob was the tool I needed.

I took his advice and read the book and finally chose saints who jumped out for me: St. Francis of Assisi, St. Augustine of Hippo, and St. Ignatius of Loyola.

My dear friend and brother went home to the Lord suddenly on November 1, 2011 (All Saints' Day) at age fifty-nine. I was visiting the sick at a nursing home when I received the news of Bob's passing. I had to end my visits and went into a bathroom stall and cried. I hadn't cried like that since my mother had passed away. I immediately returned to the church to pray for Bob. I was so upset that I wanted to stick my head in the tabernacle and yell at God, "Why did you take him from me?" I have only known Bob for about nine years, but I felt like he was with me all my life. He was and still is such an influence for me, and I still need him. I will always need him. It was only proper that Bob went home to the Lord on All Saints' Day, for I always claimed he was indeed a saint. It was also appropriate that I received my second significant healing at Bob's house.

One day, I started to feel a shortness of breath; and as the days went on, it seemed to get worse. I finally went to a pulmonary doctor who explained that I had COPD (chronic obstructive pulmonary disease), so he put me on an inhaler that didn't seem to work. One day, my breathing was so bad that I ended up in the emergency room. One of the left chambers of my heart was not working. The doctor explained in detail, "The heart has four chambers, two atria and two ventricles. There is a wall, septum, between the two atria and another barrier between the two ventricles. Arteries and veins carry blood to the heart." He believed the valve controlling my left atrium was blocked and that I would probably need surgery to correct the problem. He also explained that this was very serious because "the left atrium receives oxygen-rich blood from the lungs and pumps it to the left ventricle, which pumps the oxygen-rich blood to the body." He added that he had to correct it quickly and that more tests would be needed.

About a week later, Jackie told me that Carol De Roy was having Mass said at her home and would like for us to attend. I told her it was impossible because of the way I was feeling. But she insisted we go because the mass was for Bob and that we must attend. "Let's make a showing, and if you still feel sick, we can leave." After her continual insisting, I agreed to go.

That night, it rained so hard that the visibility was terrible. But we arrived safely at Bob's house, only to learn that the mass was not for Bob but a healing mass. Now I was extremely agitated. Dragging me out in the pouring rain while I was feeling the way I did was mean. Besides, I didn't approve of having a mass in a person's home mainly because most of them were not authorized by the local bishop. My pain began to intensify, and my breathing was heavy. I wanted to go home. But for my love for Carol, I didn't say a word.

They had a table that served as an altar in her living room and about twenty chairs set up, all filled with people. The room was full, except for several empty seats at the very back row. On the wall to my right was a picture of Bob and with that winning smile, he stared at me, saying, "Behave."

There was a priest who couldn't speak any English and a woman who would do the interpenetration. All that I could think of was where I knew this woman because she looked very familiar to me. As I sat in misery, trying to breathe and deal with the pain in my chest, I wondered how I ever let Jackie talk me into this insanity.

The priest's name was Father Tony, and he was from the Dominican Republic. The interpreter's name was Marta. Father Tony seemed somewhat queasy and uncomfortable, probably because of the language difference. But I was fixed on Marta. Where did I know her from?

They set up the makeshift altar. Just before starting the mass, Marta announced that sometime during the mass, Father Tony would sit down, and God would tell who he would be healing. I wasn't paying any attention to what she was saying; I was tuned out. All I could think of was the pain I was feeling. And who was this woman?

The mass started, but I was not participating. I wanted no part of this Earl Roberts amusement party. As she had said, at one point during the mass, Father Tony sat in a chair and looked like he was in a deep trance or was pretending to be in one. All of a sudden, he spoke, "Someone in this room has a severe back injury. I want to tell you that God has healed you."

No one in the room stood up and shouted hallelujah, only silence. Again, he claimed, "Someone in this room has a brain tumor," and added, "I want to tell you that God has healed you." Again only silence. I believed he would keep this up until someone responded. It reminded me of a television healing show where a healing preacher would call you up, place his hands on your chest, and yell, "Heal!"

He continued calling out several other health problems and still, only silence. Looking back at me, he said "Someone here has a heart problem."

Now he has my attention.

"He has a blocked left atrium," he added.

Wow! I thought someone has the same problem as me.

After the mass, as they were taking down the altar in the living room, I decided it was my time to approach Marta to inquire as to how I knew her. As I came closer, Father Tony stopped me by placing his hands on my chest, but he didn't yell, "Heal!" It was like he was protecting her from me as if I was a danger to her.

She took hold of my arm and said, "You're the one."

"The one who?" I asked

"The one he healed," she answered.

"Yeah, okay," I said. "Where do I know you from?"

Now I discovered they had food, my kind of food—donuts and all kinds of junk food—so I decided to stay a little longer. Throughout the evening, I noticed Father Tony kept staring at me, and it made me uneasy. It was time to go home. As I was leaving, I had to pass by him. He stood there, blocking my way, and again placed his hands on my chest and smiled. Only this time, I could feel a strange impression in my chest like his hand was radiating through my chest to my back.

On the drive home, Jackie asked me how I felt.

"What do you mean?" I answered.

"Well, how do you feel? How is the pain and your breathing?"

I stopped to think and realized I had no pain, and my breathing was good. I felt great.

She said, "I felt something was going to happen tonight. That priest healed you."

I guessed so. I felt great.

When we arrived back home, it was still drizzling, but I decided to walk our dog around the lake, which was something impossible just a few hours earlier. Back at the house, I was so excited that I had call Carol. Father Tony was the real thing. God had granted me a second healing.

The very next day, I had an appointment with my cardiologist. He was located on the second floor, so we had to take the elevator. But this time, I ran up the stairs. Jackie asked me if I was going to tell the doctor what had happened. I told her, "I don't think so. He is basically a scientist, so don't except such things."

I entered the examination room, and a medical assistant took an EKG. A few seconds later, the doctor came in, holding the EKG strip. "Tell me what happened," he almost shouted.

"What do you mean?" I asked.

"You needed more tests. Your left atrium was blocked almost completely, and I was sure you would probably need surgery to open it up. How, according to this strip, is your heart in perfect condition? No more blockage?"

I told him what had happen. He just stood there, looking amazed. He said, "I can't dispute this. What is this priest name? I would like to send all my patients to him."

As we arrived back home, there was a phone call from Carol. "Marta called. Father Tony is having a healing mass at a local parish and would like for you to attend to give testimony about your healing."

I answered that I would be delighted.

Chapter 5

Billy Bread

One of the last words a man wants to hear is his sixteen-year-old daughter is pregnant. Well, that is precisely what happened to me back in 1983. Returning home from work one day, I found a stranger in my living room with a young boy, almost hiding behind him. I recognized the boy as one of my daughter's friends by the name Louis.

Jackie looked sick with worry, and I knew this couldn't be good. She was afraid of my Irish temper and that I would blow out of control. Jackie asked me to sit down and prepared me for some bad news.

"Ginger is pregnant," she cried. She didn't say it clearly enough for me to understand.

"What did you say?" I asked.

But before she could answer, the stranger said coldly, "Ginger, your daughter, is pregnant."

I couldn't register this. "What did you say?" And he repeated it.

"And should I guess who the father is? And who you are?" I practically yelled.

He told he was Louis's dad, and yes, Louis was the father of the child.

I just sat and did not saying a word, trying to take all this in. For no reason, I stood quickly. He backed up like he was afraid I would hit him, but I didn't. I just lost control of my emotions and had to move. All I could think of was my little curly-haired girl, who once always ran to my arms when she saw me coming home, was now pregnant. I had to get it together, calm myself down, and think intelligently about the situation.

The stranger's dad spoke, disturbing my thinking, saying there were two options we could do: one, Ginger could come and live with them and have the baby; and two, she could have an abortion.

I angrily turned to him and said, "I will never allow my daughter to live with anyone who will even consider an abortion. Get out of my house before I throw you out."

That was the last time I ever saw Louis or his father.

We decided to move Ginger to Tampa and stay with my sister, Barbie, until she had the baby. Then we would put the child up for adoption through Catholic charities.

Time went quickly, and it was time for her to give birth, so we rushed to be with her. On May 7, 1984, my grandson came into this world. Ginger made a request to see the baby, which I was against; but she wanted to make sure the baby was all right.

Now like my own father whom I was never able to know, I had a grandson I would never get to know.

Every day, I would pray for the child I didn't know. Then one day, while praying at the tomb of Padre Pio at San Giovanni, a voice came to me. "Ginger will be all right." I didn't know what it meant, But I knew it was from Padre Pio because I had been praying to him for years for Ginger. Her life was miserable at that time, and she needed something to lift her spirit.

When I returned home, it wasn't long before Ginger called to let me know she had received a letter from the adoption agency, saying they had a letter from her son wanting to know who his mother was. She needed my advice, and I told her I had heard of this before and that it didn't always work out for good. But she had an obligation to answer the letter, which she did.

It was 2007, and the child was twenty-one years old. The mother and child started their communication by letter, and one day, he called her on the phone. He lived in Daytona, Florida, and Ginger resided in Fort Lauderdale, a distance of only 242 miles or a three-hour trip. He was now married; and his wife, Josie, was pregnant with a boy (my first great-grandson). He worked with his father who owned a bread delivery business called Billy Bread. His dad's name was William "Billy" Newborn, and his mother's name was Sandy. The boy's name was also Billy.

The communications seemed to be going very well. It was all Ginger would talk about, and I could see a joyful change in her. Thank you, Padre Pio.

One day, she decided to make the trip to meet Billy and his family, but she was extremely nervous about how she would be received by both Billy and his parents. Would there be a lot of difficult questions she couldn't answer like "Why did you give me up?"

I told her to relax and put it in God's hands, for this was meant to be. And it was. Everything went perfectly. She was well received. Before long, it was my turn to meet my grandson, and I was nervous. When Jackie and I arrived in Daytona and at Billy's house, the whole family was there to greet us. It was amazing we were welcomed like long-lost cousins. I was surprised when I looked at Billy. From the pictures I had of my father, John, he was his spitting image. He was definitely a Flynn. His wife, Josie, was beautiful and pleasant. They made us feel really comfortable and part of the family. I was extremely happy for Ginger and, I must say, for myself. All the years of praying for this child had paid off. God was good.

Billy's mother Sandra was a loving woman and most friendly toward us. If I daresay, it was almost like she was happy we came into Billy's life. I had never meet a more affectionate person. Billy's father Billy Bread, he was called, was also warm and very friendly toward us. You could tell they were Christian folks from the south and practiced what they preached. They were good people, and I could see why Billy turned out so well.

Now we were part of the family and enjoyed our many trips to visit them.

On February 12, 2008, Josie gave birth to Kyle, my first great-grandson; and on July 14, 2008, to Macy, my third great-granddaughter.

I couldn't be happier enjoying my new family until sadly, on June 5, 2012, Sandra Newborn suddenly went home to Our Lord at age sixty-three. I mourned for Sandra like she was my own sister. As I mentioned before, she was one of the decent persons I had ever meet.

My relationship with Billy Bread continued to grow, and on visits like birthdays, we would separate into a quiet place and talk. I think he liked me, and he knew I liked him, and we both loved Billy.

Again, sadly, on May 3, 2014, William "Billy Bread" Newborn also went home to our Lord at age sixty-five.

I visited my grandson as much as possible but not as much as I liked to.

What more do we need to have to acknowledge God's goodness toward us?

Chapter 6

Secular Franciscan Order

One day, as I was serving at St. Andrews, a sweet elderly woman entered my office and introduced herself as Sister Celine Buzzer, the formation director for the local fraternity of Secular Franciscans, and that she now had permission to use one of the classrooms for the formation. I told her it was nice and that if I could help her in any way, just let me know. And she did. Every time she held a meeting, she would drop in to ask for something—pencils, erasers, or turn up or down the air conditioner. But she was nice about it, and I really liked her.

I had no idea what she was teaching. It was not a CCD class or Bible study, and I had no idea what Secular Franciscans were all about. So one day, I made a mistake and asked her. From that moment on, after her class, she would stop in my office uninvited, sit down, and start explaining what the Secular Franciscan Order was all about. After several weeks of this, I was well informed.

I mentioned I had been to Assisi three times, and I had books she might be interested in to help with her classes. She appreciated the offer and asked if I would be willing to attend class and talk about my experiences. I told her I would, and that was the final nail in the coffin.

"You should attend more classes or even join the order," she kept insisting.

"No thank you. I am too devoted to St. Augustine."

But the recruiting never ceased, and as a good drill sergeant, Sister continued to persuade me to attend a meeting.

Then one day, another woman came to her class. She looked very similar, kind of like the woman my priest would hide from when he saw her coming. Her name was Mary Varvaro, and she was a handful like a little piece of dynamite. After the meeting, she marched into my office, sat down, and looked me straight in the eye, saying, "Sister told me all about you." And with a very demanding but soft voice, she continued, "Be at the next meeting."

When she had left, I had to laugh.

The meeting was exceedingly boring for me. All I could see were elderly women yelling at each other. I had no idea what was going on. It seemed that gristle, Mary, was the leader of this wolf pack, and this quiet-speaking person was about to attack.

I was so relieved when the meeting was over. I could escape safely. I vowed never to attend another meeting.

The next week went fast, and it was time for Sister's meeting. I tried to avoid her by returning to my office and felt safe once the meeting started. But to my surprise, there she was, sitting and waiting for me. "How did you like the meeting?" she asked.

"Are you kidding?" I yelled. "It was a disaster and an embarrassment to St. Francis. What are you trying to do, woman?"

To that, Sister had nothing to say, and she politely left the office. Finally, this would be the last of it. But now came the reinforcements.

In her next meeting, there was another woman, one who I recognized as Maria Rosa, a parishioner at St. Andrews. She had been handicapped from an automobile accident. Following the meeting, they were in my office. "This is Maria, a good friend of mine," Sister claimed. "She is homebound and unable to receive the Eucharist."

I replied, "if she is homebound, how did she get here?"

"I was able to drive her," she answered. "But I am unable to drive her to Mass. It would be nice if you could visit her and bring her the Eucharist."

Not knowing this was a setup, I agreed to visit Maria, not knowing she was a secret agent for the fraternity.

My visits to her were pleasant enough. She was an elderly Italian woman, and we talked about my trips to Assisi. She would always bring up the fraternity, telling me how wonderful it was and that I should give it another try. Week after week, she would sneak into our conversations the latest information and how great its members were. She claimed the meeting I attended did not represent how the normal meetings were. "You should attend another meeting."

"Why are you pushing so hard for me to join?" I asked.

She explained, "We don't just look for people join to increase our membership. Joining the Secular Franciscan Order is a calling for a lifetime commitment." She told me that as members, they were always looking for people who might have the calling. "And we think that you have the calling."

"How do I know if I have the calling?" I asked.

"We look for men and women we feel have the potential gift of becoming Secular Franciscans. That is what it is, a gift from God," she explained. "It's a feeling we have that you have that calling. Only a discernment period and prayer will reveal if you have a calling. We would like you to attend a few more meetings, and after three months, you will have a better idea if you want to continue with the formation. Three months will give you time to look us over and an opportunity for us to learn more about you. It's a lifetime commitment, not one to be taken lightly."

I decided to attend a few more meetings, considering they seemed to know something about me that I didn't. The next several meeting was interesting. I enjoyed them because I took a new interest in possibly becoming a member.

Three mounts went by fast, and I was being considered for initial formation. I passed through the orientation and inquiry period and was now assigned a formation director. I was instructed that I had to learn and understand the SFO rule, constitution, Franciscan spirituality, particular Franciscan statutes, traditions, and customs. My director spoke of a formation process that went in rotation or cycle. In other words, the bulk of the information presented during the initial formation wouldn't have a beginning or endpoint. It would be ongoing. Whenever the inquirers presented themselves and were deemed ready to begin the formation process, they would simply "plug in" to where everyone else was.

I found this to be the case in my formation. There were only two of us—a man named Carl and me. However, there was a third person named Simon who was on his third attempt at the formation. It had to be said about Simon that it was not necessarily his doing for continuance. He was a source of information during a time of a variety of changes in the order. The formation process was being updated. A new manual was being produced, and they were even changing the name of the order from the Secular Franciscan Order to Ordo Franciscanus Saecularis (Secular Franciscan Order in Latin). Throughout these changes, Simon kind of fell through the cracks, but he seemed to be on track in our little group.

The formation director assigned to us was an elderly woman who was living in the past. She was a sweet person whom I became very fond of; however, her formation style appeared to be a little contrary to what the manual was telling us. Her style of teaching consisted of recollecting things gone by. She never talked about St. Francis or fraternity life, only about old friends and places. But she did have the ability to tell us what books to read, and I developed a decent collection of books by Franciscan writers: Ilia Delio, OSF; Lazaro Iriarte de Aspurz, OFM Cap.; and Regis J. Armstrong, OFM Cap., to mention just a few. Her name was Regina, and her manner of teaching proved fruitful, for all three of us were professed into the Secular Franciscan Order at that same time. Yes, even Simon.

I learned so much by reading the books Regina had recommended that it wasn't long before I became the next formation director. The first thing I learned was that Secular Franciscans are tertiaries or members of the Third Order of Saint Francis, founded by St. Francis of Assisi eight hundred years ago.

> [2]Although Secular Franciscans make a public profession and are consecrated, they are not

---

[2]   Ladypovertyregion.org/profession-as-a-secular-Franciscan.

bound by public vows as are religious living in a community.

They make profession to live out the Gospel life and commit themselves to that living out the Gospel according to the example of St. Francis.

Membership of the Secular Franciscan Order includes lay men and women as well as diocesan priests.

Secular Franciscans should seek to encounter the living and active person of Christ in their brothers and sisters, in Sacred Scripture, in the Church and in liturgical activity. They do this by studying, loving and living in an integrated human and evangelical life.

Secular Franciscans live by a rule book consisting of twenty-six rules—simple rules that help us in living the Gospel life according to St. Francis. Most of them came from the saint himself, such as rule 13:

As the Father sees in every person the features of his Son, the firstborn of many brothers and sisters, so the Secular Franciscans with a gentle and courteous spirit accept all people as a gift of the Lord and an image of Christ.

A sense of community will make them joyful and ready to place themselves to live on an equal basis with all people, especially with the lowly for whom strive to create conditions of life worthy of people redeemed by Christ. (The Rule of the Secular Franciscan Order, 13)

In rule 5, St. Francis implies that every human person who ever lived or will live on this big beautiful blue planet is my brother and sister.

> Secular Franciscans, therefore, should seek to encounter the living and active person of Christ in their brothers and sisters, in Sacred Scripture, in the Church, and liturgical activity. The faith of St. Francis, who often said, "I see nothing bodily of the Most High Son of God in this world except His most holy body and blood," should be the inspiration and pattern of their Eucharistic life. (The Rule of the Secular Franciscan Order, 5)

I was particularly surprised when I learned it was the Mother of Christ. The saint was quoting Matthew 5:16, "For whoever does the will of my heavenly Father is my brother, and sister, and mother," when he wrote in his letter concerning those who did penance:

> [3][We are] mothers when we carry Him in our heart and body (cf. 1 Cor 6:20) through love and a pure and sincere conscience; we give birth to Him through [His] holy manner of working, which should shine before others as an example (cf. Mt 5:16).

Being a member of the SFO was something that changed my life for the better, something I took very seriously. All those things I had said back at Medjugorje that had to be changed in my life were changed. My attitude toward others, particularly toward those

---

[3]   Rule of the Secular Franciscan Order. Published by The National Fraternity of the Secular Franciscan Order-United States of America-Fourth Printing 2008. Page 2.

whom I was not too friendly with, changed completely. I could feel St. Francis's hand on my shoulder, leading me to a better lifestyle.

> The life of the Christian has three distinguishing
> aspects: deeds, words, and thoughts. The
> thought comes first, then words, since our
> words express openly the interior conclusions
> of the mind. Finally, afterthoughts and words,
> comes action, for our deeds carry out what
> the mind has conceived. So when one of these
> results in our acting or speaking or thinking,
> we must make sure that all our thoughts,
> words, and deeds are controlled by the divine
> ideal, the revelation of Christ. For then our
> thoughts, words, and deeds will not fall
> short of the nobility of their implications.
> —From a treatise on Christian Perfection by
> St. Gregory of Nyssa, bishop, 46, 283–286

Chapter 7

The Commander

Very few men in my life had made an impression and influence that made a positive difference for good. Fr. Jim Vitucci and Bob De Roy were two, and the third was Robert Earl Dimmitt, Bob, as he was affectionately called by many, but I always called him the Commander. The Commander was an extremely religious man and attended Mass as often as he could during his long military career. Once retired, he came to Mass every Sunday with his wife, Kathryn (Kitty), and daughter, Claudia. Claudia Shipman was a Eucharistic minister at St. Christopher Catholic Church, and she always served at the ten-thirty mass.

I was the sacristan for that mass, so I naturally know Claudia. But it was a real pleasure when I met her parents, Bob and Kitty. Like clockwork, they entered the church around ten fifteen to get ready for Mass. Bob and Kitty were both in wheelchairs, and I personally greeted them as they entered. They were both in their nineties.

Kitty was fascinating for her age, a beautiful woman both inside and out. I took a real liking to her. Every Sunday, as they entered, I would leave the sacristy to kiss her on the cheek. Sadly, on November 6, 2017, Kitty went home to the Lord. We were all devastated, especially the Commander. Their marriage must have been a special, loving relationship, for I never knew anyone who grieved the loss of a spouse as he did. I remember him telling me at the funeral, "You were the important one, for I was only the husband, but you were the boyfriend."

I started visiting the Commander during his short stays in the hospital and nursing homes and eventually at his house every week. I immediately took a liking to him because like my Dad, he was a war hero. He had proudly served in the navy during World War II, the Korean War, and Vietnam. He was shot down in the South Pacific and received the Purple Heart, a military decoration for those wounded or killed while serving in the military, along with the Distinguished Flying Cross, which is awarded to one who distinguishes himself by extraordinary achievement while participating in an aerial flight; and the Air Medal, a military decoration awarded to one for heroism or extraordinary action. The Commander shared his military experiences with me, a low-ranking man enlisted in the marines. He took pleasure in kidding me because I joined the marines, "a small part of the navy" and not the navy.

We spent many enjoyable hours together. And sometimes when I could, I would visit him twice a week. I started to think of him as the father I never know.

A lot of homebound patients enjoyed visits because they were lonely and appreciated anyone who would visit them. Such was the Commander. I could tell he enjoyed my visits. It came to the point that I hated to leave him. He would receive the Eucharist. I would read from the Bible, and we would discuss the passage I had read. He appeared to be very interested in the readings and sometimes would ask me to explain it in more detail as if he was searching for something that was lacking in his life that he had to make up for.

Finally, we arrived at the matter of feeling guilty for past sins and believing he was living in mortal sin. Now I was out of my element. This would require a priest to hear his confession. I knew I had to go slowly now. He hadn't been to confession in a very long time, and I would say, "Oh, you have to confess your sins before you can receive the Eucharist again. At this point will be destructive." I consulted a priest friend on how to go forward. He said he "needs the Eucharist to have the Holy Spirit work in him" and that I "should continue to read the Bible, looking for passages that applied to his situation."

I would prepare well for my visits, searching the right passages and researched them until I memorized them. I prayed and asked the Holy Spirit to help me and be with me as I visited the Commander. I started to realize perhaps this was why I was healed. This would be my ministry.

As I mentioned before, when Jesus gives you a job to do, he also gives you the tools to complete the job. That is so true! The Holy Spirit played his part with the Commander. All the right words were spilling from my mouth, and it wasn't me saying them.

The Commander showed a genuine likeness toward me; as a matter of fact, he would often tell me he loved me. I believe it was the Holy Spirit and not me whom he loved.

His biggest fear was he was not going to heaven to be with the love of his life, Kitty. I assured him he was going to heaven and that God loved him and forgave all his past sins because they were all venial, not mortal. He answered, "I hope so, but how do you know?"

I read to him Romans 10:19, "If you declare with your mouth, 'Jesus is Lord,' and believe in your heart that God raised him from the dead, you will be saved. You do believe this, don't you?"

"Yes," was his answer.

"Well," I said, "it must be true because there is only one thing I know that God can't do."

He looked puzzled and asked, "What is that?"

I answered, "He can't lie."

Again, he said, "I hope so."

After several more meetings with me using Bible quotations that fit his situation, I decided it was time for my friend Fr. Joseph Torretto to hear his confession.

On my next visit, Father Joe heard the Commander's confession and explained he was not in mortal sin at all and probably never was.

On my next visit, there was a noticeable change in the Commander. He looked more peaceful and relieved. We talked again about his going to heaven and being with Kitty, and this time, he didn't say "I hope so" but "I know so."

This would be my last visit to my friend the Commandeer, for on November 22, 2017, he went home to his enteral rest and reward and to be with our Lord and the love of his life, Kitty.

I remained friends with Claudia, who was almost family, and I believe both the Commander and Kitty rejoiced with that.

Chapter 8

Father Joe

Of all the wonderful and devoted priests I'd known in my life, the one who stood out to be the most influential for me was Fr. Joseph Torretto, a priest from the Richmond diocese. I first met Father Joe when I was serving the hospital ministry. He was a patient. At first, I was concerned about entering the room because I had never prayed for a sick priest in person before. When I entered the room, I found a personable, friendly person who was somewhat surprised to see me.

"I have been in this hospital for four days, and no one from the church until you have come to visit me." he said."

"I am surprised to hear that," I said. "Usually, the hospital informs the parish when a Catholic is admitted. Besides, you are on my list to visit."

There was another person in the room whom Father Joe introduced as Carlos, a seminarian studying for priesthood.

I started to feel relaxed around Father Joe and promised I would revisit him, which I did several times. I introduced him to Father Jack, and soon he was celebrating Mass at St. Andrews. Joe was preparing for retirement from his parish in Martinsville, Virginia, and had already purchased a condo in our area. He would visit Florida as often as he could, and he soon started filling in for Father Jack when he went to Medjugorje.

One day, Father Joe asked me if I would like to visit Carlos with him at the seminary. I was delighted, and that started a custom that lasted for over twelve years. Once a month, Father Joe and I would drive to the seminary to support young men studying for priesthood. I was amazed at Father's devotion and financial support for these young men. Naturally, Father and I became friends and spent more time together, and I realized he was a generous person with anyone he knew who were in need.

As time passed, more and more, I admired Father Joe. He patiently listened as I complained about almost anything and everything. Our relationship grew, and we became more like brothers than friends.

Eventually, he retired and moved to Florida permanently, and now we see or communicate almost daily.

Father Joe was an excellent influence for me, most influentially being his teachings about Pope John XXIII. Father was a graduate from John XXIII. Father Joe's devotion toward the Good Pope was passed on to me. I read many books on the life of John XXIII, which led me to a detailed studying of the Vatican II documents.

One day, Father Joe surprised me by saying he would be going to Rome for the canonization of Pope John XXIII. But more to my surprise and shock, Jackie and I would be going with him and that he was paying all the expenses. I couldn't believe it, but it was true. All I had to do was drive to Boston and meet up with Father Joe, who was visiting friends. Along the way, I was to go to Chancellorsville, Virginia, to pick up another friend of Father Joe who would be traveling with us. Her name was Barbara, whom I had the pleasure of meeting several times while visiting Father Joe in Florida. Many of his friends also became my friends.

Jackie and I were very excited about preparing for this adventure, and although we had been to Rome before, this trip was special because of the canonization of both Pope John Paul II and John XXIII. And to make it more unique, we would be traveling with seminarians from John XXIII Seminary, which meant we would also be going with Cardinal Sean Patrick O'Malley. It couldn't get any better.

The April day finally arrived when we would start the long drive to Boston. We had recently purchased a new car, which added to the excitement. Besides, we hadn't had a real vacation for several years, so we were both in high moods as we headed north. Chancellorsville was beautiful, and since it was Good Friday, we stayed at Barbara's for three days and headed for Boston on Easter Sunday after mass.

Arriving in Boston, we hooked up with Father Joe at the hotel and enjoyed a nice dinner and a much-needed night's rest. The next day, we had to be at the airport until evening, so we spent the day visiting another friend of Father Joe, whose name was Dave, and his wife, Pat. They lived in Medford, the town I grew up in. Dave took on a tour of the city where naturally, I didn't recognize anything, except St. Francis of Assisi Catholic Church, my childhood parish. We also visited the John W. Flynn Ice Skating Rink, named after my father.

Dave also drove us to the airport where we met up with the group from the seminary. Cardinal O'Malley was already in Rome. However, there was an auxiliary bishop. Father Joe introduced him as Bishop Peter J. Uglietto. He was amiable. Sometimes it was hard to think of him as a bishop because he was so pleasant.

The overnight flight was long and uneventful. We were unable to sleep. I watched movies I had seen before.

Arriving in Rome, we were met by our travel agent who let us through customs. Up to this point, everything went smoothly, but now things started to fall apart. Outside the airport, there was a line of buses waiting for passengers. As we walked past the buses, admiring how nice they were because they were new-looking with comfortable seats and a coffee maker, we were expecting to board the same style of comfort. But as we passed the long line of modern buses, we arrived at an older-looking one that was ours. There was no coffee maker.

We traveled through the beautiful Italian countryside for several hours before arriving at Assisi, the birthplace of St. Francis. Pulling up to a nice hotel, our agent went to check us in. Gone for about a half an hour, he came and boarded the bus. We were at the wrong hotel. Finally, we arrived at the right hotel though not as lovely as the wrong hotel. We were assigned rooms. Father Joe and I couldn't find the air conditioner, so I returned to the desk to inquire how to turn it on, only to be told they didn't have air condition. We had to open the window.

Next, we were to assemble outside for a walk to Chiesa Nuova, the home of St. Francis. A church had been built on top of the place where St. Francis's house was.

We were being led by a local tour guide who was new at the job and not very knowledgeable of the area. She led us to the steepest hill I had ever climbed; it was almost straight up. Everyone was hurting and not happy, crumbling, and trying hard to breathe. Halfway up, our legs started to hurt. Finally, we reached the top, only to find we were at the wrong church.

It was a good thing we were a religious group because if looks could kill, this tour guide would be dead a thousand times.

Back at the hotel, I couldn't sleep. My legs hurt so bad, and with the open window serving as an air conditioner, all I could hear were neighborhood dogs barking all night.

The next day, we visited the Papal Basilica of Saint Mary of the Angels located within Portiuncula, a small church where the Franciscan movement started and the cell where St. Francis died.

It was unclear if we would tour the basilica before the mass or after. By now, the frustration started to show on Father Joe's and other friendly faces. I became upset, thinking we might miss and not have the time to tour Portiuncula properly, which was, to me, an essential site to visit while in Assisi. Being here several times before, I was familiar with the area. I suggested we walk, but they wanted to wait for the bus. Only Father Joe said, "Let's go."

It was a pleasant short walk through the ancient village, and upon arriving, we found the basilica to be not very crowded. We had plenty of time to tour Portiuncula and pray at the site where St. Francis died. It was a beautiful spiritual experience.

It was 10:45 when the bus arrived, and the rest of our group was rushed to a chapel for the mass, not having the time to tour the basilica at all.

The next day, we were back in the bus, heading for Rome. There was some excitement on the faces of the group. However, there was also some frustration and disappointment because of the last few days in Assisi.

Arriving in Rome promised much of the same as in Assisi. The hotel was not as promoted that our hotel would be within walking distance from Vatican and that we would have a view of St. Peter's Square from our rooms. It didn't. The hotel was located way past Castel Sant'Angelo and was quite a distance from Vatican. The crowds were unbelievable. It seemed like everyone from Poland was here for the canonization of Pope John Paul II. Groups of people walked from Poland. I couldn't believe this until I returned home and check it out on the internet. There were people everywhere in sleeping bags or were hanging out in restaurants. I couldn't ever remember seeing or being in such a crowd before. You could tell they were poor people. The tourist attractions were not bad; it was just trying to get to them.

We did get to tour the Colosseum and Castel Sant'Angelo. But when we went to Vatican, it was a disaster. The lines were so long, and the crowd was too dense to see anything. We were herded like cattle through the Sistine Chapel without being able to see anything. Tempers started to flare, and I could see the anger on Father Joe's face. He was agitated. He wanted to see the open casket of Pope John XXIII. We stood in a long line that wasn't going anywhere. He decided to step over the roped-off area and find it himself. I decided I better follow him to see what jail they would put him in.

I was greatly surprised that as we made our way toward the Papal Altar, no one tried to stop us. Now we were standing behind the altar, just the two of us, looking for John XXIII when a man in uniform—probably a policeman—signaled for us to come to him. It was all over. Both of us would spend the next five or ten years in an Italian prison.

The officer led us to a door with stairs going down. It must have led to a holding cell, but it didn't. Now we were in the grotto underneath the main floor of Saint Peter's and was ushered into a small chapel filled with people waiting for a mass to start.

Naturally, we stayed for the mass, which was celebrated by a cardinal who didn't speak English. After the mass, as people were leaving the chapel, turning to the right, Father Joe turned to the left. Amazingly, we were now in the grotto, looking at the tombs of popes and saints. We came across the site where John Paul II's tomb lay and eventually the empty tomb of John XXIII. Being disappointed by not finding the tomb, we decided it was time to go back to the group. We came across a door with a sign in Italian and hopped it was an exit. It was.

Outside, I was relieved we weren't arrested and still amazed we were able to do this. The guards must have been very busy handling the vast crowds.

So far, everything concerning this trip was a disappointment, especially for Father Joe. He was looking forward to being here, but the money he had spent only turned out like this. I could see the frustration building up. But the worst was yet to come during the day of the canonization.

Traveling with a group from the John XXIII Seminary, we were told that a section of St. Peter's Square was assigned us. However, we couldn't possibly get to Vatican. Several members left at 6:00 a.m., only to return at 9:00 a.m., claiming they could only go two blocks from the hotel. We ended up watching the canonization on television in Italian.

You could cut the tension in the group with a knife. It was a good thing we were a religious group, or who knows what would come out of our anger. It was terrible; everyone was silent and not talking to each other. When you are that angry, you take it out on the people near you, and that's what we did. All four of us seemed to be upset with each other and wouldn't talk. If we did, it was in an angry tone, saying things I knew we didn't mean. I felt sorry for Father Joe for his disappointment and accepted his harshness.

The flight back home was a relief. We sat separated from each other, and I was hoping we would all cool down by the time we would arrive back in Boston. But the frustration still existed; and the drive to Chancellorsville to bring Barbara home was a long one, filled with tension and, thank God, a lot of silence. By the time we arrived back in Florida, attitudes started to change by placing our anger where it belonged—on the travel agency—and not each other.

We realized the things we said we didn't mean, but no apologies were necessary.

Sometimes, true friendship is put to the test. The four of us remained friends, and our relationships are still growing to this day and, I guess, at times put to the test.

Chapter 9

Fr. Justin M. Russolillo

Some people attend daily mass regularly that no matter what is going on in their lives, they will never miss a mass. I deeply admire such people and wished I had faith like that.

One such devoted parishioner was a woman named Erna. She was always in prayer and was silent. It was very hard to get to know her because you never wanted to disturb her while she was praying. One day, she came up to me and started talking to me. Out of the blue, she told me her uncle would one day be canonized a saint.

I was astounded and didn't know what to say, so I said, "Tell me all about him."

This silent, saintly woman told me everything about her uncle. His name was Justin M. Russolillo, an Italian Roman Catholic priest and founder of both the Vocationist Fathers and the Vocationist Sisters. Father Russolillo had gone home to the Lord in 1955.

I became so interested in this Italian priest, so I kept asking Erna to tell me more about him.

As time went on, Erna supplied me books and anything she had on her uncle. She even gave me a first-class relic: a piece of clothing with a button he wore. I placed it in a necklace and wore it around my neck.

I became so devoted to this saint and prayed to him every day so much that I could feel his presence in my life like a guiding angel protecting me, especially when I ran myself over with my car.

One day, a friend asked me to take him to the hospital because he was to have some test done that required someone driving him home. I was only too happy to help. Once we arrived at the hospital parking lot, there was no parking available because of construction going on. We were unable to find a place to park, so I decided to drop my friend at the main entrance of the hospital. I then circled the parking lot until found a space to park. After several trips around the lot, I noticed a space on the next aisle. As I turned toward the space, another car behind me rushed around me and took the space. I was extremely provoked at this, but I keep my cool. People are very strange today. If I confronted the guy, I might get shot, so I let it go. Besides, another space was becoming empty as a large pickup truck started to back out.

Looking out his window, he saw me waiting with my blinker on. He gave me a big smile and retook the space. I figured he was playing a game with me and would give up the space. He played this game several times, and I just sat there, getting more and more provoked. Now several cars were lining up behind me, and they also were aggravated. Some started blowing their horns and yelling at me.

The man kept playing his game, and I noticed he was drinking liquor from a bottle. I had to do something. The nut in front of me wouldn't move, and the nuts behind me wouldn't stop blowing their horns. I was so upset. I had to do something. I decided to face this nut head-on, which was very silly of me to do. I should have just driven on and forget about it, but I was so ravaged by now that I was freaked out and not thinking right. I let my anger control my actions.

As I started to get out of my car, I didn't realize I put the car in reverse instead of park. Besides that, there was a metal manhole cover that I stepped on that was still wet from last night's rain. As I started to exit my car, my foot landed on that wet metal cover, and down I went. I landed in a prone position on my left side. I was not hurt. My left foot was flat on its side. Suddenly, the car started moving backward, rolling completely over my left foot. I could see the car lifting up and down over my foot, but I felt no pain. I could hear a woman screaming as she witnessed what had happened. She screamed even louder when I stood up because they thought the car ran over my head.

What happened was the car ran over the midsole of my sneaker, which was the strongest part that protected my foot. It was a miracle my foot wasn't crushed because I would be crippled for the rest of my life. I stood and trying to stop the car from rolling backward. It was heading toward another car. All my efforts and strength failed, and my car backed into a parked car, causing minor damage ($3,000).

The screaming woman who thought I was dead with a flat head called 911. There I was in a hospital parking lot, and they called 911. A panicked-looking policeman rushed to me, asking me if I was all right. "Yes," I said, "but my car's not."

After explaining what had happened, he looked at me very strangely and said, "I don't know how to write this up. Let me understand this correctly. Your car ran you over.

"Yes," I said.

He continued, "And you are not hurt?"

"Correct," I said.

He asked me if I was married. When I told him yes, he said, "Do you want me to come home with you to explain this to your wife?" As he looked down and continued to write in his pad, I heard him laugh to himself in a soft tone. "I can't wait to tell this to the boys back at the station."

This was indeed another amazing event in my life and another example of how God guides and protects us. The image of Father Justin stuck in my brain, and I do not doubt the Holy Spirit acted through Father Justin that day to protect me.

There are so many dangers around us that can hurt us at any time. I believe God is protecting us every second of our lives. Sometimes he works through others, deceased family members, and loved ones and, yes, all the wonderful saints in heaven.

Chapter 10

My Hawaiian Girl

For it will not be you speaking, but the Spirit
of your Father speaking through you.
—Matthew 10:20

Now at my advanced age in life (the twilight years as they say), I can look back and realize all the times God was with me, guiding and protecting me (which was all the time). He never left my side. I also realized this when he sent people to me who needed his help through me to get back on the right track. As I reflect on this, there are many. One such person was a young mother named Denise.

Denise and her husband, Bobby, moved to an apartment in the building next to ours. The couple had two delightful children, a boy, Bobby Junior, and a precious little girl named Lanai. I took a particular liking to this family, especially Lanai, whom I called my little Hawaiian girl. She loved ice cream, and I made sure every time I would go to the store, I would always remember to buy her ice cream. I cherished the look on her face when I gave it to her.

It went on for years as I watched them grow up. I would sit on my patio and watch them playing, riding skateboard or bikes, or just running around the lake. Young Bobbie was good at fixing bikes. He would find them at the trash bins, bring them home to fix them up, and then sell them. I remember walking past his garage and seeing him working on an old bike. He always had three or four in the garage. He was quite a young businessperson.

Lanai was a lovable little girl with fire-engine-red hair just like my daughter, Ginger, had at her age.

Bobby was a chef who seemed to have a hard time keeping a job. However, he appeared to be a friendly guy who was always there with a helping hand. Bobby and I would meet at the pool and talk while the kids swam and had a good time. We became good friends.

Denise was always quiet and kept to herself. At that time, I didn't get to know her, only what Bobby had told me about her, which were good things. He built her up as a good mother, and they appeared to be a happy couple.

The more I got to know Bobby, the more concerned I became. He was kindhearted and friendly, but some hidden emotions started to submerge, and I started to see a different Bobby. I became alarmed when he started telling me about all the weapons he had. I was never satisfied with people having a lot of firearms around children, and according to Bobby, he had plenty. The more I listened to him, the more I felt he was making things up and trying to impress me. But I was not impressed. I was also concerned about his religious belief, which I couldn't understand but respected. I would inquire more about his faith, and he told me his faith was on his arm. All the tattoos he had represented a different aspect of his religion. I respected all religions and tried to find more information on the internet but was unsuccessful.

As our friendship continued, Bobby seemed to change. He became more dispirited and was provoked about something. I never asked. I only listened.

Then one day, he told me he was divorcing Denise. I was shocked and distressed. A separation would always mean the relocation of one of the parents, usually the father. I was also worried that if Denise moved, I would lose my friendly relationship with my little Hawaiian girl. There was nothing I could do. I could and should not get involved, but Bobby kept seeking me out to complain about his failing marriage. It was as if he needed someone to talk to, but it wasn't intelligent conversations where I could reply with angelic advice based on my more than fifty years of successful and loving marriage. It was all ridiculous, one-sided reasons for leaving such a beautiful family, and he was not giving any thought on how this would affect his children. I felt he was doing this for selfish reasons. I liked Bobby, and I valued our friendship, but I couldn't understand why he was doing this.

I told him not to berate his wife anymore because I didn't know her that well, but I admired her and felt she was an excellent mother to his two children. I asked him to try to remember why he married her and how he loved her very much, that instead of considering separation, he should communicate with her and try to rekindle that loving relationship they once had or even find a marriage counselor.

I started to think there were other reasons for his actions he wasn't telling me, and realized I was wasting my time trying to advise him. He didn't care and was using me to let out his anger and frustrating.

Our talks started to dawdle when I made it very clear I wouldn't listen to any negative comment concerning Denise.

That dreadful moment finally arrived when Bobby told me he filed for divorce and was moving out this weekend. I was sad to hear this because Denise would also be moving, along with Bobby Junior and my Hawaiian girl. There was no sense in talking to Bobby. His mind was made up, and there was nothing more I could say that would change it. He did move, and I would only hear from him when he complained about the divorce procedures. I was glad when he stopped calling me altogether.

I went to the pool or walked the dog around the lake more often, hoping I would see Bobby Junior and Lanai playing. I wanted to enjoy them as much as I could before they moved away.

Then the day came when Denise told me she was moving, but they were moving to the apartment above mine. I could not be happier, and all Lanai could say was "Great, more ice cream!" I couldn't be happier; all I had to do was sit on my patio and watch them coming and going.

They appeared to be content in their new apartment, and Denise was doing an outstanding job raising them as a single mom. They called me Mr. Bill, and I was glad to have them say hello.

It wasn't too long before Denise was dating a fellow named Andy. Andy was an honorable person who didn't hesitate to tell me his past marriages and that he was still married to his second who lived in California. It was definitely none of my business, and I couldn't understand why he was telling me all this. I didn't know what Denise told him about me. Perhaps he wanted to talk to someone to get this off his chest and clean the slate before starting a new relationship, which he took very seriously. And I was a good listener.

I must admit I was concerned over his confession. I didn't want Denise to rush into another relationship and end up getting hurt again. But I had no say in this and had no right to say anything at all. I was not a relative and had no authority over this family. I was just a friend who knew what happened and genuinely cared for this family.

As time went on, I had many more conversations with Andy, and I developed a liking toward him. He was a good man, and we became good friends.

The next several years passed quickly, and the kids grew into impressive adolescents—Bobby, a fine-looking tall teenager with his bright-red hair; and Lanai, a beautiful preteen, also tall for her age and, yes, charming with her long fire-engine-red hair. I couldn't believe how fast they grew, and I would tell Denise to stop feeding or watering them. Denise and her children added to my happiness in living in this apartment building.

One day, as I was walking my dog, I heard the loud sound of fire engines heading toward our apartment building. As they came closer, the sirens got louder and louder until they arrived in front of my apartment. I became very nervous. What could have happened to Jackie? Perhaps she fell but was able to call 911.

As I rushed toward the fire engines, more trucks arrived plus several police cars. Now I started to panic. What was going on?

Then the fire and police officers rushed upstairs to Denise's apartment. Something must have happened to Denise because the kids were still in school.

Jackie was standing on our patio, watching. I quickly joined her, wondering if Denise was all right. Suddenly, there was a loud knock on my door. It was a police detective asking who I was. When I told him, he said, "Andy said you are the family minister, and he needs you to come upstairs."

I told him I wasn't a minister. Perhaps Denise, not fully understanding my religion and my status in the church, believed I was a minister because of my past involvement in counseling her during her divorce proceedings.

"That doesn't matter," the detective said. "He thinks you are, and he needs and wants you now. Please come upstairs."

Not aware of what he wanted, I agreed.

Upstairs, surrounding Denise's door stood a lot of police. Out came Andy, looking terrible, shaken, and pale white. "She's gone," he cried.

"Who's gone?" I asked. "Denise?"

"No," he said, "Lanai. She committed suicide."

It could not be true what he was telling me. I lost control of my emotions and started to cry myself. It could not be possible. My little Hawaiian girl… I sat on the stairs, trying to register this in my mind while crying my eyes out.

School had just started about two weeks ago, and last week, Lanai wasn't attending classes. A friend of Denise's who worked at the school called her to inform her of her absence. Denise called Andy to check on her. Arriving at the apartment, he discovered Lanai and called 911. A detective sat next to me, putting his arm around me, trying to console me. He said I had to be strong for this family because they needed me. "And we need you to tell Denise of this horrific tragedy."

"What? Are you insane? Don't you have professional counselors for situations like this?"

"Yes, we do, but they are strangers. It will be best if someone she knows and respects tell her, and right now, that person is you."

"Yes," I agreed, "but how do you tell a mother that her twelve-year-old daughter had committed suicide?"

He said that Andy had just called her at work, telling her to come home quickly. "She must be aware that something awful had happened. We want you to meet her at the gate and stop her from coming to the apartment."

For some reason, beyond my understanding, I agreed. I was incoherent and afraid I might say the wrong words and make matters worse.

As I walked toward, the gate I prayed intensely to the Holy Spirit for help. I could hear the Holy Spirit telling me to be at peace with this. "For it will not be you speaking, but the Spirit of your Father speaking through you." I immediately became relaxed and was able to compose myself.

Denise came running and crying toward me. She hugged so tight like she was never going to let me go. I could hardly breathe. I started talking to her, and words of comfort and compassion flowed out of my mouth. They were words I couldn't remember because it was the Holy Spirit speaking through me. This was an occurrence that never should have happened to me or anyone, telling a parent they lost a child by suicide. But it was an occurrence I have learned from. It's not about us; it's about God.

I don't know why or understand why a child will commit suicide. But God made me a part of this tragedy to show me that the Holy Spirit does work through us. I wished he had shown me differently. He allowed this to happen for a reason that I will never understand until I am with him in heaven. "And we know that all things work together for good to those who love God, to those who are called according to his purpose" (Rom 8:28).

I can never forget Lanai (a new angel in heaven) or her family that brought much joy in my life, if only for a short time. This was only one of the many graces God worked through me to comfort others. For this gift and many others God has granted me, I am extremely thankful for. I will never stop being amazed at how he works through us. I am inflamed with love for Jesus because he changed my life and overwhelmed by his mercy.

Lanai is now in the sweet embrace and loving adobe of paradise, in the arms of a loving Father in heaven. And in my heart, she will live forever.

I lost contact with Denise and Andy when they rented a house and moved away. We also decided to move back to Fort Lauderdale to be closer to our grandchildren. The move was hard for me, being away from my parish and Father Hynes and the many friends I had made over the years. But it was good for Jackie to be closer to the family, and it was time for a change in me. Besides, we were getting older, and we needed to be closer where the family could help if needed.

We found a cozy little apartment just five minutes from my grandchildren and settled in. It had a lovely community, and I enjoyed walking my dog, Jack, and seeing all the beautiful trees and shrubs.

Did you notice the dog's name is the same as my wife, Jackie?

It happened like this. Our lovely little Chihuahua, Toby, that we had since a pup, had passed away. I told Jackie no more pets for a while. Well, that lasted for three days, and we adopted a beautiful red-and-white papillon. He was the friendliest dog I had ever seen, and he took a liking to Jackie. He was definitely the best dog we ever had. But there was only one problem: he came with the name Jack, and at seven years old, that couldn't be changed. It all seemed to work out, except at times, when I would tell Jack to go lie down, Jackie would tell me she wasn't tired.

After a while, we adopted a cat that we named Jill. Now we have, Jack and Bill and Jack and Jill. Sounds confusing, it is.

In closing, I wish to thank you for allowing me to share my life with you. No matter what your illness or health conditions are, remember: miracles happen every day. Never stop praying to God, and keep him close in your heart and soul.

I will never understand why I receive so many graces, and until the day he tells me why he loves me, I can only keep thanking him for a life worth living.

Even if the life of a person has been a disaster,
even if it is destroyed by vices, drugs, or
anything else, God is in this person' life.
You can, you must try to seek God in
every human life. Although the life of a
person is a land full of thorns and weeds,
there is always a space in which the good
seed can grow. You have to trust God.

—Pope Francis

About the Author

William S. Flynn was born in Medford, Massachusetts. He struggled in school and finally quit in the eighth grade to enter the marines, only to achieve in later life a college degree in biomedical engineering.

He is presently living in Florida with his adoring wife of over fifty years, Jackie, and their adoring dog, Jack.

CPSIA information can be obtained
at www.ICGtesting.com
Printed in the USA
FSHW011224120421
80287FS

9 781098 047054